To Jeanette & Charleen,
With best wishes —

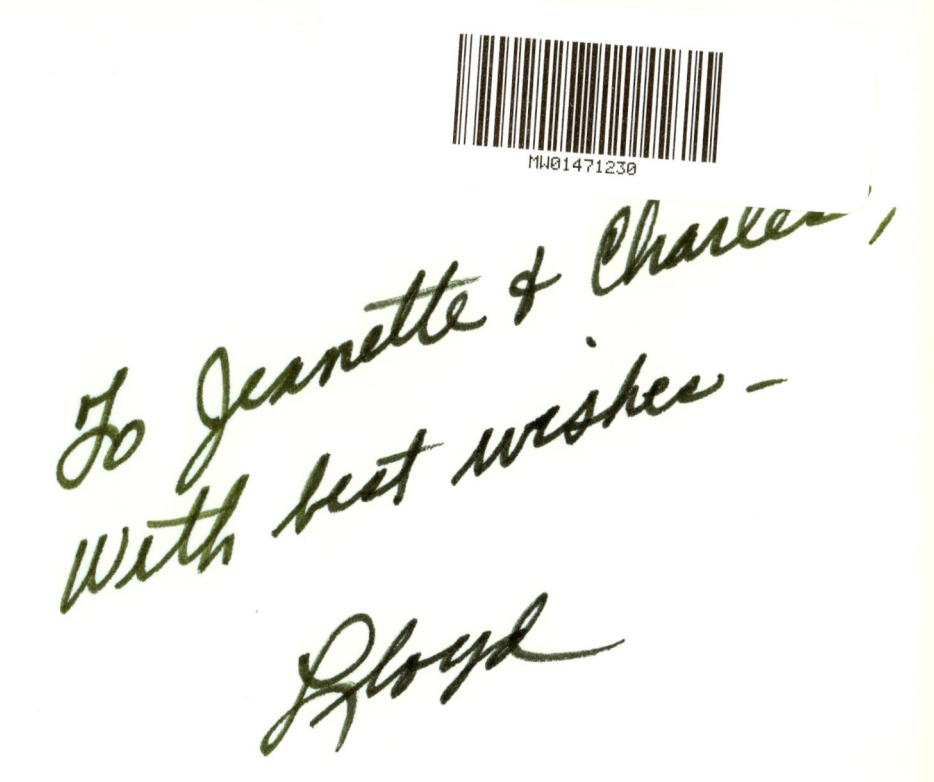

Lloyd

SUMMARY JUSTICE
A Story Of Revenge

SUMMARY JUSTICE
A Story Of Revenge

Lloyd J. Guillory

Rutledge Books, Inc.   Bethel, CT

Jacket images © 1996 Photo Disc, Inc.

Copyright © 1996 by Lloyd J. Guillory
ALL RIGHTS RESERVED.

Rutledge Books, Inc.
8 F.J. Clarke Circle, Bethel, CT 06801

Manufactured in the United States of America

Library of Congress Cataloging in Publication Data
Guillory, Lloyd J.
   Summary justice / Lloyd J. Guillory
     p. cm.
   ISBN 1-887750-05-3
   1. Murder -- Louisiana -- New Orleans -- Fiction.
2. Detective and mystery stories.   I. Title
813.54 -- dc20   95-71268

THIS BOOK IS A WORK OF FICTION. THE CHARACTERS AND SITUATIONS IN THE STORY ARE IMAGINARY. NO RESEMBLANCE IS INTENDED BETWEEN THESE CHARACTERS AND ANY REAL PERSON, EITHER LIVING OR DEAD.

Summary Justice

CHAPTER ONE

NEW ORLEANS FRENCH QUARTER - WEDNESDAY MORNING

As the taxi pulled to the curb in front of the main entrance to the Royal Orleans Hotel, the lone occupant in the rear seat looked in all directions, as was his custom. He was a cautious man. He had to be. He was an assassin, a contract killer.

He exited the cab and glanced at the old empty Civil Courts building across the street and admired its Greco-Roman exterior. With his European background he favored classical architecture over the plain monotony of modern buildings. The doorman rushed over to take his bags, consisting of one military style B-4 type and an oversize briefcase. He allowed him to take the B-4, but not the briefcase, and then turned to give the driver his tab plus a fifteen percent tip. He was cautious never to over or under tip—either was reason to be remembered and he never wanted to be remembered by anyone, not even his clients.

He entered and climbed the marble steps to the main lobby level and turned right to the registration desk after a quick perusal of the entire lobby. The clerk gave him the required smile, asking, "May I help you, sir?"

Like most Europeans, he spoke several languages, and due to determined effort he spoke five with barely a discernible accent. He had difficulty in not rolling his "r's" as do most natives of the Mediterranean, so he tried to avoid words with the letter "r". He replied, "My name is Nicolas Bono. I have a reservation," and he was careful with the "r".

"Ah, yes, Mr. Bono ... a one-bedroom suite with a bath. Is that correct, sir?"

He nodded. He never talked when he did not have to. He took the offered pen and filled in the blanks, all with lies and misinformation.

The clerk looked at the form, asking, "And how would you prefer to pay, sir, cash or credit?"

Without an audible response, he removed a billfold of travelers checks from his inside jacket pocket. He signed two one-hundred dollar

1

checks and handed them to the clerk, who responded, "Very good, sir. I'll give you a receipt for the money and we will balance out when you check out," and he snapped his finger for a bellhop.

The man handed the B-4 bag to the bellhop and carrying the briefcase, followed him to the elevator bank. He paused in the elevator lobby, looking at the small marble staircase leading to a lower level. Turning to the bellhop, he inquired, "Where do those steps go?"

"To the lower level, sir ... small shops and to the parking garage."

He nodded and headed into the open elevator and as the cab moved upwards responded to the bellhop's friendly comment: "Nice day, isn't it?" with a short: "Yes."

As they exited the elevator he looked in both directions and saw that the corridor ended at a dead end, with another suite at its end. He smiled inwardly. It was just as it was described to him in his instructions. Their room was at the end of the corridor. He followed the bellhop into his suite and taking the bag from him, gave him two one-dollar bills, then followed him to the door and closed it behind him. He waited a few moments and walked out into the corridor, looking furtively in both directions. It was mid-morning and the early check-outs had already gone and the late sleepers were not yet stirring. He walked to the elevator lobby and viewed the required exit plan posted on the wall. He studied the floor plan and noted the location of the exit stair wells. Satisfied, he returned to his room and began to unpack the B-4 bag. He carefully removed his trousers and jackets and hung them in the closet. He was proud of his clothing. He bought nothing but the best. It was one of his few weaknesses. He liked good clothing and he traveled first class. He could afford it. For the past few years, since he had acquired an international reputation for efficiency and professionalism, he had averaged over $250,000 a year—tax free. He claimed no country as his own and owed none his allegiance. He had several passports, each with a different appearance and name, for he was a master of disguises.

His usual "extermination" fee, as he euphemistically referred to his craft, was $25,000 per individual, except for industrial and corporate exterminations, which were negotiated on an individual basis. His present assignment called for the demise of two people, a man and a woman. He requested his usual $25,000 per, but his booking agent informed him that the client had balked on the basis that they would both be in the same place—in bed—and that if he caught them in the correct position, he could kill them both with one bullet. In his twisted mind, that amused him, but he negotiated on the price of $37,500. Besides, it was to be his last job of the current year and he was ready to leave for his annual month's vacation on the French Riviera.

Summary Justice

After his clothing had been hung, he reached into one of the side pockets of the bag and withdrew a small, flat box, opened it, and removed a black wig, a black beard, a tam of the type that European men wore, and a thick pair of eyeglasses made of plain glass. He placed his briefcase on the table and opened it. It contained his pride and joy. His eyes shone with fondness as he ran his fingers over the breakdown rifle, a Belgian Mauser which fired a .257 Roberts cartridge. With its 4 power scope, was deadly at several hundred years. He lifted the .38 caliber, six-shot revolver and caressed it. Some assassins preferred automatics, but he preferred the revolver. He could see at a glance how he stood on ammunition. The case also contained two matched throwing knives when quiet was essential and required. Each weapon rested in a molded foam rubber recess and required only half the thickness of the case. A dividing cover, when in place, allowed room for his theatrical disguises and a black jacket of poor construction. Satisfied, he closed the case and went into the bathroom. After relieving himself, he stood before the mirror and admired himself, as he often did. He was proud of his professional skills and reputation, as he thought of how he came into the business. Born in the back country of the hills of Sicily into a poor family named Buonarroti, he was christened Nicola Guiseppi Buonarroti. His bestial father, who liked to boast that they were distant relatives of the great Michelangelo Buonarroti (which could not be confirmed), made a meager living as a "goffer" for the local Mafia soldiers, far down from the bosses in Palermo. His father abused him, his mother, and systematically raped both his older sisters, who had left home at the ages of thirteen and fourteen. Their fear of him was exceeded only by their hatred. After one exceedingly drunken beating of his mother, she subsequently died from it and was secretly buried by the father in their backyard.

It was then that he plotted to kill the father. He was only twelve at the time, but was driven by a combination of fear and hatred. While the father was asleep after one of his drunken orgies, he quietly and without much emotion, cut his throat with a table knife. He dragged the body to the backyard and buried it adjoining his mother, but, in deference to her hatred of her husband, he buried them feet to feet. He felt his mother would have preferred it that way. Terror stricken at his own deed when the fury had died down and knowing that his father's brothers, his uncles, would kill him in revenge, he left for Palermo and the waiting arms of the Mafia who could always use a young man with killer instinct running from the law. He was trained by the best and he became one of the best.

As he viewed himself in the mirror, he saw a man in his mid-thirties, in robust health, slightly under six feet in height, an athletic build, with hair close cropped, smooth olive skin, and a Roman nose. As he smiled, an even set of white teeth framed by full lips were visible. He shook himself out of his reverie and, picking up his briefcase, walked out into the corridor. He made his way to the exit stair, proceeded down to the parking garage and exited on Chartres Street. He walked east, not wanting to pass in front of the main entrance on St. Louis where the doorman could see him. He walked over to Bourbon and then proceeded west until he came to the Holiday Inn. He cautiously waited outside the public restroom until he was sure it was empty. He entered and went into a toilet stall and locked the door. He extracted the wig and beard and with theatrical glue pasted them in place. He placed the tam on his head and the thick glasses on his eyes. He then took off his custom made jacket, gray in color, carefully folded it and placed it in the space in the case from which he extracted the cheap all black jacket. Having put it on, he closed the case and left the toilet stall after determining that the rest room was still vacant. He stopped only long enough to check himself in the mirror. He smiled, pleased with himself. He looked like any Middle Eastern native—Lebanese, Jewish, Iranian. "What did it matter?" he thought. Americans could not tell one from the other. He quietly exited the Holiday Inn and made his way back to the Royal Orleans, but not before stopping at a hock shop to purchase an old, used suitcase. He placed his briefcase in it and made his way to the main entrance of the hotel.

The doorman watched him come along Royal and then cross over St. Louis. He knew that tips would be meager from this man who resembled a political refugee just off the boat, but in true Southern fashion, the black doorman smiled, opened the door, and said, "Mornin', suh. Nice day, ain't it?" He nodded and managed a smile. He climbed the stairs to the main lobby and proceeded to look around nervously in practiced fashion. He wanted to be noticed this time. He wanted to be remembered by all who saw him. He made his way to the registration desk where the clerk, who looked him up and down, had difficulty managing a smile as he asked with some disdain, "May I help you, sir?"

With as much accent as he could muster, complete with rolling "r's", he responded in broken English, "I have rrresrrvation forrr two nights."

"Your name, sir?"

"Name is Emile rrrRashid."

Perusing the computer screen, the clerk was surprised to discover that indeed, the reservation had been made. He smiled more easily this time as he replied, "Yes, sir. We are holding one single for you for two nights. It that correct Mr. Rashid?"

"Yes, yes," he replied nervously. "Eees corrrect."

Turning the registration form to him, the clerk asked: "And how would you prefer to pay for this, Mr. Rashid, cash or credit?"

He extracted a small leather pouch from his pocket and produced two one-hundred dollar bills, asking, "Eees 'nough?"

The clerk smiled inwardly, replying, "Yes, sir. That should cover the length of your stay. We can balance out at check out time. Your key, sir. Enjoy your stay."

The bellhop attempted to take the bag, but without success, which did not surprise him or the clerk. As they watched the man shuffle off, they looked at each other with the bellhop jesting, "There goes a big spender."

He made his way to the gift shop, purchased a USA TODAY, and made his way to the seating area to read it. He passed a plain clothes hotel security man standing there watching him. He could spot security men in a crowd. He purposely went up to him, asking him the time. He wanted the security man to know he was a guest of the hotel. It was vital to his plan. He sat and read the paper without real interest and feeling sure he had been seen and noticed by at least a dozen people, he went up to his room, the small room of Emile Rashid. He now had registered in the hotel under two different names and had exhibited two different personas. His plan was going well.

He went to the bed and messed it as though someone had had a fitful night in it. He went into the bath and used several towels and face cloths to simulate room occupancy by a messy person. He removed his disguises and returned to the dress and appearance of Nicolas Bono. He carefully opened the corridor and seeing no one in the hall, he went to the elevators and up to his first suite. He saw the cleaning women in the hall, still working some of the rooms. He went into his bath, extracted the towels and hid them in the closet. He then went into the hall and told one of the cleaning women he had no towels and he was ready to take a shower. She seemed genuinely surprised for she had seen her assistant come out of the room just a few minutes before, but she knew better than to argue with a guest, so she apologized and took two towels and went into his room, followed by him. He struck up a conversation with her in her native Spanish, in which he was completely fluent. This surprised and flattered her. He asked her pertinent questions concerning the time they cleaned the floor, usually, in case he wanted to sleep late the next morning, he explained. She cheerily volunteered all he wanted to know. He gave her a five dollar bill, and having six children at home, all under the age of ten, she took it, gratefully. He wanted her to remember him on this occasion. It was part of his plan.

Today was Wednesday and the couple he intended to kill would not be checked in to the hotel until the next day, Thursday. They had a pre-arranged liaison each first and third Thursday of the month at the same time in the same hotel. How stupid, he thought. Repetition is deadly. Habits can kill you. If they were dumb enough to meet on a regular basis, why not change their time and location, and why pick a high profile hotel like the Royal Orleans? Why not some second-rate motel out in the country? There had to be a reason, he felt, but it did not matter to him how stupid they were, or, why they had offended someone so much that they wanted them killed. All that mattered was that they did want them killed and they were willing to pay him $37,500 to do it, in unmarked, used one hundred dollar bills. He mentally went over his plan and feeling he could not do any more that day, he took the rest of the day off to enjoy the pleasures of New Orleans, the most European of American cities. He thought of indulging in his own libidinous lust but he changed his mind. It was not a top priority with him, and it had never been. He felt like St. Paul, grateful it was not a problem with him, and on those infrequent occasions when he did feel an urge to satisfy his cravings, he did so in a businesslike fashion. He hired the best he could find, paid them well, and sent them on their way. It was done devoid of tenderness or emotion of any kind, for he had none. He held the human race in contempt, never trusting anyone enough to form a relationship of any kind, man or woman. He was aware of his own shortcomings but it never bothered him. On the contrary, he felt without them he would not be the successful assassin he had become. Emotions were a sign of weakness, and he liked to think he had no weaknesses.

He showered, dressed, and then went down to the lobby. He handed his room key to the desk clerk. He wanted them to know he had left. He walked down the back stairs and exited the hotel through the parking garage. He proceeded to the Jackson Square area and spent several hours walking among the artists plying their trade, trying to interest tourists in some of their paintings. He walked across the street to the Cafe DuMonde and watched the procession of people who came to partake of coffee and beignets. He was fascinated by the human race, even if he did hold it in contempt. He studied people, constantly. The more he knew about people, the easier it was to kill them when he had to. He felt people were weak and stupid, bumbling through life, making the same mistakes day in and day out.

He walked up the Moon Walk and then proceeded to walk the river walk all the way to the new aquarium, which he toured. The sharks fascinated him—one of the world's most efficient killers. Now, there was an animal he could admire. Tiring of it all, he returned to his room and lay in bed, studying photos of his intended victims, complete with physical descriptions. The man was fifty-four and the woman was thirty-two. He smiled a twisted smiled and thought, "And tomorrow will be the last day of their lives. I hope they enjoy it!" He decided that he would not kill them right away. He would allow them to have some fun, first. He was proud of his generosity.

The next morning he awoke early, as he always did on one of these days, his adrenaline pumping. After all the killings he had done, he thought it would be routine by now, but it wasn't. It still thrilled him each and every time. He recalled a recent corporate assignment in Europe. Some irate stockholders wanted the C.E.O. removed from his job; there was a corporate insurance policy on his life for five million dollars, and the firm needed the money. It was necessary to explode a Lear jet in mid-air with five other people on board. That was one of the few times he had remorse of conscience, but, he reasoned ... c'est la vie!

He dressed in his own clothes and then went down to the small room of Emile Rashid. He locked the door and proceeded to transform Nicolas Bono into Emile Rashid. Like a great stage actor, he enjoyed the making up nearly as much as the play. He ceremoniously placed each disguise on his person with theatrical flourish, and when he had finished, he proceeded to remove it all. It was only a dress rehearsal. He placed the disguises in the case and checking the revolver one more time, he transformed himself back into Nicolas Bono. He picked up the briefcase and went to the door, cracking it a little. Some people were in the corridor and he could not afford to be seen exiting that room as Nicolas Bono, so he waited until they had gone into the elevator. He then took the next elevator to the lobby. He walked around the lobby for several minutes to be seen, then he reentered the elevator and went up to the suite floor. Right on schedule the maids were working the floor. The one to whom he had given the five dollar bill the day before greeted him with more than usual affection, in Spanish. She told the other two Hispanic women how nice that gentleman was, and they exchanged some innocuous words, all in Spanish. He left them and went into his own suite, which they had already cleaned. He timed it carefully, watching as they eventually opened the door to the suite of the intended victims. He allowed them to make up the suite, and while the door was still opened, he went to the maid to whom he had given the money. He told her he had a medical problem which required an ice pack and asked if she would be so kind as to get him some ice. Just as she gladly responded, he informed her that he had to go to the drug store in the gift shop to get some medicine, and that he would not be there when she returned, but, to just put the ice in his room. His request was accompanied by another five dollar bill. She protested mildly that already he had been too generous. He told her she reminded him of his mother and he could not be too generous to her. He loved all mothers. Deeply touched, she wiped tears from her eyes, and walked to the ice machine area around the corner, leaving the door to the suite open, which was precisely what he wanted and needed.

Seeing her disappear around the corner, he quickly entered the suite and closed the door. The suite was identical to his, so he was familiar with the arrangement. He quickly hid in the closet in case a maid had to come back for some reason, but after some time had elapsed, he felt safe in coming out. He glanced at his watch. It was only 10:35. The couple's rendezvous time was always 2:00pm, he had been told. It would be a long wait, but he had no choice. At least he was in the room with no one, especially hotel security, having any reason to believe he was.

He exited the closet and went in to the bathroom with his briefcase. He transformed himself into Emile Rashid in short order, having remembered each motion from the dress rehearsal. He carefully looked around to ensure that he had not disturbed anything in the bath, and then proceeded to the closet. He left one closet door open and sat on the floor, briefcase beside him. Carefully removing the revolver, he checked it one more time, then settled down for a long wait. He dozed off and on, and then looked at his watch. It was 1:45pm. The time was drawing near. He did not know if they were punctual people, or not. He also did not know if they came together or separately. He did not know much about them, but it made no difference to him. He knew one thing, that although he planned to kill them in bed, if either of them decided to hang their clothing in the closet he would have to kill them at will, as best he could.

He screwed the silencer onto the barrel of the revolver. He was as ready as he could be. He felt his breathing increase in intensity and frequency. It always did that, he remembered, but he tried to calm down. He heard a key slip into the lock. He quietly closed the closet door and had to depend on noise to tell him what was going on in the room. It did not take him long to tell it was the woman who had entered. He could smell her fragrance, obviously put on extra heavy for the occasion. He heard her walk across the room. His breathing became harder as he feared she might open the closet doors. Instead, she made her way to the bathroom. He could tell by the sound of the high heels on the tile floor. He slightly opened one of the closet doors. He could now see her in the bath, looking into the mirror. He felt sure the angle was such that she could not see the closet doors. She began to remove her street clothing until she was only wearing panties and a bra. His heart skipped a beat as she exited the bath, feeling sure that she intended to hang her street clothes in the closet, but she didn't. She placed them on the back of a chair. She extracted a sheer negligée from the large hanging purse she had carried in and returned to the bathroom. With her back to him and facing the mirror, she completely disrobed. In the mirror, he had a full frontal view of her. She was a beautiful woman with a slender, lithe figure and ample breasts that defied the laws of gravity. Even he could understand how a man, foolish as he was, could lose his head over her. For just a moment he could feel his own libido aroused to the point that he wished he had availed himself of the French Quarter's many opportunities the previous night.

She stood there for a moment, admiring herself in the mirror. She disappeared to the area of the commode, which he could not see. He heard it flush. She returned and put the negligée around her. She went to the TV set and turned it on, louder than she should have. He was grateful to her. He welcomed the loud noise for reasons different from hers. He smiled. Evidently, she was a screamer, he thought. She went to the bed, turned back the bed covers and climbed in. Propped up on her pillow, she proceeded to flick through channels as she waited. At exactly 2:05, he barely heard the door open again, and he knew the other half of the assignment was coming in. Through the cracked door he could see the man go to the bed. He sat on the bed and kissed the woman passionately. He stood up, said something indiscernible over the TV noise and headed for the bathroom. He exited in a minute completely nude, without shame. Obviously, they felt at home with one another in the nude. The man was trim and well built for his age. Probably he worked out regularly. She made room for him in bed and they lost little time in getting to the matter at hand. He now knew why she had turned the TV up louder than usual. She was, indeed, quite audible in her enjoyment of ecstasy, not spasmodically, but continuously. Whether this was due to unbridled passion or for effect, he could not tell, nor did he care. After allowing them to enjoy what would be their last moments in this world, he quietly began to rise from his sitting position. He could not deny that he had enjoyed the spectacle to some degree, himself.

His breathing decidedly quickened as he slid the door completely open. So enthralled were they in their passion that he did not even have to move carefully. He could feel the adrenaline flowing madly through his veins as he walked slowly toward the bed. They had just rolled over, once again, so that she was now on her back. It was she who first saw the bearded stranger peering at her through thick glasses, gun in hand, walking toward the bed. She stared with horror-stricken eyes as he aimed the gun at her head. Before she could scream, he pulled the trigger and the bullet entered her chin. The man turned his head in amazement as her head flew back from the impact of the bullet. He half attempted to turn his body when the second bullet entered the back of his head, exiting the front and carrying half his brain with it. It was done in a fraction of a second. He had earned his fee. They lay there, each soaking the clean white sheets with red. He watched them for a moment, then, feeling each for a pulse and finding none, he slowly backed away, still watching them. He unscrewed the silencer and placed the weapons in the briefcase. He went to the door, turned to give them one more look, then hesitated as he mulled over two options.

He returned to the area of the bed, looking down at his victims, then, he went to the chair where the man had placed his clothing. Still wearing the surgical gloves, he removed the man's wallet from the rear pocket. He slowly opened it and found three hundred and sixty dollars in cash and two gold credit cards. He frowned as he extracted the cash and credit cards and threw the billfold on the floor. He went to the dresser where the woman had removed her jewelry. He saw a gold bracelet, a wedding ring, two diamond earrings, and a large diamond ring, all of which he placed in his pocket. He found this thievery highly distasteful for a professional man of his international reputation. It brought him down to the level of a common thief, but he had decided that it was the most viable of the two options—to leave them or take them. If he had left the valuables untouched, the police would know that the motive was not robbery and they would open a more expanded type of investigation, a revenge killing, something he would prefer to avoid if at all possible. With the valuables so obviously removed, the police could not help but think it was a case of simple robbery. But, the killings! Were they necessary? Yes, his reasoning concluded. The police would assume that the victims had seen the robber and would be able to identify the killer, so he had no alternative but to kill them.

Satisfied that he had exercised the best option, even if it meant indulging in common thievery, he returned to the door, took one last look, and removed his surgical gloves, using one of them to turn the knob. He placed the "DON'T DISTURB" sign on the doorknob, then made his way to the elevator and upon seeing the door open, he observed the two couples already in it. Perfect, he thought. Future witnesses have seen Emile Rashid getting into the elevator on that floor. As the elevator reached the lobby floor, the two couples exited, taking no further notice of him. He was alone in the elevator, now, and he punched the buttom for the floor of Emile Rashid's room. Once in the room, he quickly removed the disguise and once again became Nicolas Bono. Emile Rashid no longer existed. He went down to the lobby, exited the hotel and walked to the Cafe to have a cup of coffee.

The next morning, he flew to Memphis, then to Boston, then to Madrid. He flew all legs of the flights under different names. He left a trail virtually impossible to follow.

CHAPTER TWO

New Orleans's major newspaper, *The Times-Picayune*, usually spoke in a low-keyed and subdued voice, granting large headlines only to matters of war and peace. But this day, Saturday, the day after the discovery of the blood splattered bodies in the suite of the Royal Orleans Hotel, broke its tradition with a glaring headline: PROMINENT ARCHITECT MURDERED IN LOVE TRYST. The sub-heading, only a little less prominent, was added: Killed In Bed With Alleged Mobster's Girl Friend.

To the staid and prestigious old New Orleans architectural and engineering firm of Gervais & Stern, Architect/Engineers, it was a scandal which rocked the firm to its foundations, for its leading partner, Marcel Gervais, had been the victim. Bad enough that he had been killed in a most compromising of situations, but to have been killed in bed with the well-known girlfriend of one of New Orleans' Mafia heirs was more than the firm and its friends could accept with grace. The firm, in addition to doing outstanding work, was often referred to as the "Rock of Gibraltar" of design firms in the area. It had been around for more than half a century, having been founded by the fathers of the two principal partners, Marcel Gervais and Irving Stern. It was the talented and artistic Anatole Gervais, along with his brilliant Tulane classmate, Isaac Stern, who had combined architecture and engineering in the early part of the century, to found what would eventually become a premier firm in the design of buildings and bridges—an unusual combination of art and science. To most architects, engineers lacked the artistic sensitivity to become architects, and to most engineers, architects lacked the understanding of the immutable laws of physics to become good engineers. It was easier to mix oil and water than to mix architecture and engineering, but as the pragmatic Isaac Stern told his future partner, "It will work if we keep our noses out of each other's business, except as necessary." And he added, smiling, "Besides, I've never met a Cajun who could handle money with any degree of success. You need a good Jewish boy to handle the money while you supply the art."

Marcel Gervais preferred to call himself a Cajun instead of a Creole, as did he aristocratic wife, and in reply to her persistent questioning on the subject, "Why, Marcel? Why do you persist in saying you are not a Creole when your genealogy indicates that you are?"

"Because, my dear, historians have never agreed on the exact definition of a Creole, while there is no doubt as to what a Cajun is. My father arrived with the Cajun migration of 1755, so..."

"But, your mother's family came directly from France, so ... " They would argue that issue until it was no longer a point of contention now that he was gone. But to the new widow, Elsbeth Regina Cartier Gervais, there was no doubt that she was a full-blooded Creole. She was well known as a New Orleans belle from the old aristocracy that had ruled the city for two centuries.

There are three kinds of money in New Orleans: *l'argent vieux* (old money), to which Elsbeth Regina Cartier Gervais belonged; *the nouveau riche* (new money) which included most of the entreprenurial fortunes of oil and real estate running rampant in the city those days; and everyone else. There was a pecking order to be sure. L'argent vieux would associate with the nouveau riche, but with some disdain, knowing full well they, the old money, were truly superior in breeding and heritage, no matter what the true facts might be. The nouveau riche were more than happy to associate with the L'argent vieux for in New Orleans, they ruled the social roost, regardless of who had the most money. And, of course, the only avenue open to the others, the middle class was to work hard and aspire to become nouveau riche, for their ancestors had already missed the opportunity to become l'argent vieux and the opportunity would never return.

It is necessary to place each of the partners in his particular category, for in New Orleans social strata is not only important, it is immutable. Marcel Gervais, under the mantle of his wife's unimpeachable Creole heritage and her family fortune, was duly certified old money, in spite of the fact that the firm's success over the years had made him wealthy in his own right. Irving Stern, the son of one of the most successful engineers in the city, but certainly not qualified to be classified as a Creole, was classified as new money. It never bothered either man, for in the final analysis, as Irving Stern often teased his partner, "Marcel, mon ami, money is money, no matter the age," to which the partner replied, "How true, mon ami!"

Theirs was a close relationship, but only in the office and in business. The friendship never extended to their social lives for reasons neither man could have explained, except to say: "We seem to live in two different worlds." But on this day, the day after the tragedy, Irving Stern

Summary Justice

was a sad and distressed man. His partner had been brutally murdered, and under the most embarrassing of circumstances. As he told his wife on the phone, "To think he was killed in bed with a whore, nothing more than a Mafia whore." He thought of the damage it would do to the firm's image. He shrugged as he stood alone in his fifteenth floor office, looking over the city's skyline, a skyline he and Marcel Gervais had helped shape. The firm's phones were ringing off the wall with calls coming from all over the nation—some offering genuine condolences, others morbidly curious and wanting either confirmation or additional morbid details. He had told his secretary to take messages. He did not want to talk to anyone, not just now. He knew he should go to call on the widow; it was the only decent thing to do, but what could he say? What could he reply when she asked the inevitable questions, "Irving, did you know anything about this? How long has this been going on? And, with that kind of woman? My God!" He knew she would ask those questions in her imperious manner and he had no answers to comfort her. The truth is, he had known something was going on. He tried to question his partner on several occasions about the suite the firm kept at the Royal Orleans, an expensive suite ostensibly reserved for out-of-town clients, but used most frequently, lately, for Marcel Gervais's own personal use. Irving Stern, being a gentleman of the old school, had not even discussed his suspicions with his own wife, but to himself he often said, "For what other purpose could it be?" and he would add, "Marcel, Marcel, don't you see it can only lead to trouble, or worse, disaster?" But he kept these feelings to himself. He always felt that a man's personal business was just that—his personal business—unless it reflected on the firm, and now it had. He had no idea what the total effect of the disaster would have on all their lives, except that it would be traumatic. He walked to his desk, standing there for a moment just fingering things, shaking his head. Finally, he walked out the door and into his secretary's office. "Rose, I'm going out for an hour or so. I must pay a call on Mrs. Gervais."

Rose, who had worked for him for more than twenty years and knew his moods, could read the concern and distaste for the obligatory visit. She inquired, "Will you be back before lunch?" As he walked off without looking back, "No."

The stately mansion on St. Charles Avenue had been in Elsbeth's family prior to the Civil War. Her mother before her, and later she herself, had made modern improvements to include all the technology of the times. It was a large house, two and a half stories, the top floor half-story having been the living quarters for the live-in servants in those glorious and long past days when such domestic help was readily available. Now, the "help" of most families in that district of New Orleans came on the street cars still ambling along the avenue.

The house's white clapboard siding of painted heart cypress and its columned portico glistened in the late morning sun. As he pulled to the curb along St. Charles, Irving Stern felt his stomach wrench and his recurring ulcer burned in him. Such was the distaste of his visit. He glanced up the curved entrance drive filled with the cars of family and friends, all bidding for their solemn moments with the bereaved widow and her two daughters. Climbing the brick steps to the porch, Irving made his way to the impressive front entrance doors with their beveled glass lights set in a mahogany frame. He pressed the door bell beneath the brass nameplate emblazoned with the name of his partner—GERVAIS. The door was opened by a gray-haired black woman, portly of figure, dressed in the standard gray and white uniform. She had served the Gervais family for many years as maitre'd and supervisor of the other household help, which consisted of a maid, a cook, and a gardener. But she answered only to her mistress and master, and now...

Upon seeing the partner of her late employer, she assumed the required solemn appearance, shaking her head, saying, "Oh, Mista Stern, ain't it awful? Come on it. Miz Elsbeth's in the pawlah wid all dem people come to pay deh respects. Come in...."

He patted her on the shoulder with genuine compassion, for he knew her sorrow was heartfelt and sincere. "I know, Martha, it is so sad, such a tragedy." He could see Elsbeth Gervais holding court in the parlor, surrounded by a host of friends and relatives. He glanced in her direction, asking, "Do you think Mrs. Gervais could spare me a few minutes to allow me to pay my respects?"

"Oh, Yassuh, Ah'm sho she kin. Just wait heah a minute," and she ambled off.

He cleared his throat, nervously, as he looked around the oval-shaped entrance foyer with its beautiful curved stair to the upper floors. It was mostly for show, for the family generally used the back stairs which led from the kitchen directly to the bedroom area on the second floor. The curved wall held an impressive array of paintings of illustrious ancestors of both the Cartier and Gervais families. No doubt about it, he thought, this was indeed a pedigreed family on both sides. He watched as the widow rose, excusing herself from the surrounding group.

He could hear her say, "Please excuse me, I must speak with Mr. Stern, my husband's ... " and she caught herself, correcting it to ... "my late husband's partner."

He felt he should walk toward her though he wasn't sure what he would say to her. He and Elsbeth had never established a warm relationship in all the years he and her husband had been partners, due to some degree because he and Marcel had not been social friends, but also because he had perceived her to be a cold and standoffish woman. He suspected she might be anti-Semitic, but in any event, now all that was moot. He wondered, should he embrace her as close friends do, or, should he merely shake hands.

She solved the problem for him by extending her hand, saying, "Irving, how thoughtful of you to come." He later remembered mumbling something or other, hopefully, appropriate, but he was not sure. She took him by the arm and led him into the library, closing the door behind them, and signaling to a couch near the fireplace, she took a position at one end while he took the other.

She dabbed at her swollen eyes with a lace handkerchief, sniffing ever so lightly as she began, "Irving, this may not be the most propitious of times to broach this matter, but," and she sniffled again, "I must know ..."

He looked at the still handsome woman, who in her prime had been one of New Orleans' most beautiful women. Her marriage to Marcel Gervais had been the wedding of the year in a city that prides itself on elaborate ceremonies of that type. He did not let her finish, instead, interjecting, "Elsbeth, I want to tell you how sorry I am about Marcel's untimely and tragic death ... so tragic," and he shook he head. She coldly interjected, "and so unnecessary, too."

"Thank you for your sympathy, Irving, but it is the circumstances of his death that I wish to discuss with you, if you don't mind."

He felt he knew where she was going with this, and he was not happy about it. His worst fears had been realized. He placed his hand on hers, asking, "Are you sure you want to discuss this now, Elsbeth?" She dabbed at her eyes, sniffing, "Yes, I must. I have to know, Irving."

"But, I don't know any details of the..."

Her eyes lit up a little as she responded, "Of what, Irving? Did it have a name? What would you call it? An affair? A harmless dalliance with a trollop? What was it, Irving? That's what I want to know. I have to know!"

He shook his head sadly, "I swear to you, Elsbeth, I don't know what it was. I didn't know the woman. I never met her. He never mentioned her to me."

She sat upright, in the imperious and haughty manner she used when she wanted to make a point. "Do you mean to tell me you knew absolutely nothing of this woman and my husband's relationship with her?"

To this man who barely ever looked at another woman with sensual thoughts in his mind, Elsbeth's questioning embarrassed him. He shook his head, raising his hands as if in futility, "I swear, I knew nothing."

"And the hotel suite where I understand, now, he had a liaison twice a month? You knew nothing of that?"

"Well, of course, I knew of the suite. The firm kept the suite on a permanent basis ... for out-of-town clients and in-town clients as well. We used it for public relations."

She shrugged, "Is that what they call it nowadays? And whose idea was it to retain the suite—yours or my husband's?"

He answered, cautiously. "I'm fairly sure it was a joint decision. It would have to be, Elsbeth. We're talking a great deal of money each and every month..."

"I'm sure! But, who first broached the subject of the suite, in spite of the fact it was mutually agreed upon?"

He looked down at the floor, avoiding those plaintive eyes, and reluctantly replied, "It was Marcel who first suggested it."

"Well, now, isn't that interesting, that my husband who had access to this huge and beautiful home with several spare bedrooms would require a hotel suite to entertain out-of-town clients when he had brought them here for years and years. Don't you find that interesting, Irving?" and she began to cry again, softly, dabbing her eyes.

He tried not to nod in agreement, but those were his sentiments, exactly. He had presented the argument to his partner the first time the subject was broached.

She pressed on. "Were you never suspicious as to the true intent of the room?"

"I never knew what the intent was, other than what I've told you. I didn't know there was any other intent," and he added, "Elsbeth, I'm sure there will be a police investigation of this tragedy. Perhaps we should wait on that to answer these questions."

She arose to go, replying, "Perhaps you're right, Irving. This is not the time nor the place. I apologize for bringing it up, now, but ... "

He patted her shoulders: "I know, I know. We all want answers."

She nodded. "Thank you for coming. I must get back to the parlor, and please forgive my bad manners. Would you like some coffee, Irving?"

He pointed to his stomach, shaking his head. "No, thank you. The ulcer, you know."

She nodded, extended her hand, and then walked off.

As he reentered the foyer, Martha was waiting for him with his hat, holding the door open. He glanced toward the parlor where Elsbeth Gervais had resumed court with a new group of late arrivals. He returned his gaze to the maid, asking, "Martha, when the funeral arrangements are complete will you, or someone, call me to tell me of the time and place. Inform Mrs. Gervais that the office will be closed until after the burial ceremony. Would you do that, please?"

"Why, sho nuff, Mista Stern."

He thanked her and went out into the bright sunshine, threading his way among the many automobiles clogging the crowded driveway. He walked under the great oaks that lined the avenue, making his way to his automobile. Looking back at the impressive house in that magnificent neighborhood, he shook his head. "Why, Marcel, why? You had everything a man could want in this world. Why in God's name, why?"

CHAPTER THREE

The police chief was as nervous as only a call from the commissioner could make him. The commissioner had been nervous and verbally abusive as only a call from the mayor could make him. The chief sat there, chewing on a cigar butt, staring at the picture of the mayor on his office wall. The captain sat close by, nervously, as the irate chief continued to chew on the cigar, breathing hard. Finally, the chief turned to the junior officer, "Did you get the drift of that conversation, Monahan? I just got my ass chewed out because of the murder."

The captain shifted in his chair, trying to act nonchalant, replying, "Hell, Chief, we have a murder in this town every day, maybe two or three. Ain't nuthin to git too excited about."

The Chief gave his junior officer a disgusted look. "Not just any murder, you jackass, *the murder*. You know damn well what murder Ah'm talking about. This is not a murder of some whore killing her pimp over some crack cocaine. We're talkin' about a real blue-blood murder here. Marcel Gervais was a hell of a wheel in this town and city hall is some upset. They want action and they want it fast and Ah'm turning up the heat on you, Monahan! It happened in your precinct ... it's your baby, so what the hell do you intend to do about it? City Hall is asking me for answers and Ah'm askin you."

The captain shifted in his chair. He was nearing retirement and he did not need this major murder scandal at this time. He licked his lips, avoided the chief's burning gaze, and cleared his throat. "We'll try to solve it, Chief, like we always do ... "

He was rudely interrupted. "That ain't good enough, Monahan! City Hall knows you *intend* to solve the case, if you can," he emphasized sarcastically. "Right now, they want answers to give the press and especially the bereaved family. You know damn well Mrs. Gervais serves on some of the biggest commissions in this town, including," as he pointed his finger at Monahan, "the Police Department Overview Commission."

The captain swallowed nervously, nodding in agreement. "I'll put my best man on it."

"And who might that be?"

"Fortier. Michael Fortier. You heard o' him, Chief. He cracked the rape and kidnapping case of that Tulane student last year. You know him by the name of Mike Fortier, maybe. That's what the news media called him."

The chief stroked his chin. "Oh, yeah, Ah remember him ... did a damn good job on that case ... good detective work as Ah recall."

The captain nodded, proudly. "Yeah, that's him ... good man, family man, working for promotion."

"Yeah? What's his rank now?"

"Sergeant."

"Well, Monahan, you tell Mike Fortier, that if he cracks this case and cracks it soon, Ah'll see to it that he makes lieutenant. Now git the hell outa heah and solve that damn case, you hear me? And, Monahan, keep me informed on a daily basis. Remember one thing: The more heat Ah git from City Hall, the more heat you git from me!"

Monahan stood at the door, grateful that the meeting was over. He never took the chief's tirades too seriously. That was the way the Chief always talked to him, but this time, something told him that he meant it. As Monahan walked off, he muttered to himself, "Damn, I hate blue-blood murders. They're always a pain in the ass. Give me a good ole street punk killing any day. Nobody gives a damn about street punks, good riddance, but blue bloods and tourists—that's different. The news media and city hall get real excited over them as if they were different."

Mike Fortier's phone rang at his crowded desk. He motioned to the street hooker he was interviewing to cease her endless chatter as she complained that her pimp had cheated her out of some money. He picked up the phone, listened as his lieutenant gave him explicit orders, "Fortier, git your ass in heah ... now!" "Yessuh, coming right now," and turning to the hooker, "Look, Susie, you have to settle your differences with your pimp as best you can. I have more important business to take care of."

"Oh, Mike, you're just like all the rest of them. You only take care of us girls when you need us."

He looked at her with amazement. "When the hell did I ever need you? You know I don't fool with whores. I'm a happily married man ... you know that."

"Oh, I know that, but you remember when your cousin came in from

19

St. Louis ... I show'd him the time of his life and at half the going rate, too ... remember?"

As he rose, "Oh, yeah, I forgot about that. OK, look Susie, I got to go. I'll call your pimp! I'll get your money."

"You promise me, Mike? I trust you, you know."

"Sure, sugar, I'll lean on him a little ... he'll pay."

"You won't hurt him will ya?"

"Aw, no! I'll just tell him I'll put a permanent kink in his love tool—that always does it," he chuckled.

"But, you won't really do it, will you? I love him."

"That's your problem, sugar ... got to go ... bye."

As Mike neared the glass enclosed cubicle that comprised his lieutenant's office, he could see the captain talking and he had his finger in the lieutenant's face, so he figured the news was not good. He had, of course, heard of the big murder—who in New Orleans hadn't. It was in their district, and he had been disappointed when he had not been chosen to make the original inspection of the murder scene. He loved solving murders. That was what he wanted his specialty to be. He wanted to be a great detective like his retired and legendary uncle, Alcide J. Guilbert.

As the lieutenant saw Mike approach, he waved him in, "Mike, you know Captain Monahan, I'm sure," to which the junior officer replied, "Sure, good to see you, Captain."

The captain offered his hand. "Hi, Mike, good to see you. Please sit down. We want to talk to you."

That made him nervous. Captains don't usually ask junior officers to *please* sit down. All you generally got was a finger pointed to a chair if you got to sit at all.

The two senior officers looked at each other then, the captain looked at Mike. "Mike, you know the department's got a real hot potato on its hands. One of the city's leading citizens gets his brains blown out in bed with the girlfriend of the local Mafia Don's baby boy, and to say that the news media and city hall are upset would be an understatement. You'd think we were responsible for Marcel Gervais' choice of a pastime and a playmate. But, what the hell, that's what we're here for. That's what the taxpayer's pay us for, right?"

He nodded, still nervous. He wanted this case in the worst way, but he thought it was already gone. The captain continued, "The heat is on from city hall and police headquarters. The powers that be want answers and they want them fast. Any fool can figure out that this is no normal killing of a man and his broad. Marcel Gervais could have had his choice of half the women in this town, so why a Mafia cutie? And why was she

Summary Justice

killed? If the girl's boyfriend was pissed at someone trespassing on his turf why kill the loved one, too? No, Mike, this thing is more complicated, believe me, my boy, and I want you to solve it."

His eyes lit up as if he had won the lottery. The Captain continued, "We in the department," and he nodded to the lieutenant who nodded back in agreement, "have had our eyes on you. We think you have the making of a good detective, maybe a great one, like your uncle Alcide Guilbert."

Mile could hardly believe his ears. Praise like this from the Captain who hardly returned his "good mornings" when passing in the hall, but, there it was, he had said it. He tried to look modest as he suppressed a smile. The captain continued, "So, this baby is yours. The department is behind you. We'll give you anything you need in the way of support. Just solve this damn case, Mike, and the Chief promised you a promotion to Lieutenant."

His jaw dropped. His eyes brightened. He could not suppress a smile, as he rose in excitement, "Gee, Captain, that'll be great. Wait till my wife hears that," and as he turned to leave, reality set in as he asked, "but what if I can't crack the case?"

Shaking his head the captain replied, "Mike, I'd rather not talk about that, really. Now get to work."

He could hardly contain himself as he drove his Taurus station wagon in the narrow drive that separated the small shotgun houses that lined the tree-shrouded street just two blocks off Carrollton Avenue in what had been a decent neighborhood some thirty or forty years back. Now, half residential and half commercial, it was not one of the city's best, but it was close to Jesuit High School, and he hoped that his children could someday go there. The neighborhood and school was the best he could hope for on a policeman's salary in a city that had good and expensive private schools in profusion. His wife met him at the kitchen door with a cold beer and a kiss. They had married after their high school romance convinced them they wanted no others; a marriage which had now lasted twelve years with only a minimal amount of arguing and dissension, and had produced two children, both boys.

"Hi, sweetie," she greeted in her usual manner. "Have a good day?"

He returned her kiss, accepted the beer, took her by the arms, and asked, "Where are the kids?"

"Down the street, playing with the Dawson kids ... " He said with a gleam in his eyes, "Yeah? How long will they be gone?" as he reached for her. She laughed, evading his grasp. "Not that long, I'm sure. Can't it wait? Are we celebrating something? We always are when you get that look in your eyes. It's a holdover from man's early days when he came home with a mastodon under his arm, or something," she giggled. "Now, what happened today to put a smile on your face and a craving in your loins?"

"Oh, baby, I got myself a first-class murder case, that's what. The captain, himself, just gave me the Gervais case, that's what!" he remarked, proudly.

"Oh, honey, if that is what you want, then I'm happy for you, but is a grisly murder case anything to really be happy about ... really?"

As he sipped on the beer, kicked off the shoes, and removed his shoulder holster, (which she took from him with disdain, placing it on the kitchen counter), he replied, "Hell, baby, I didn't commit the murder. I'm just going to solve it." And as he smiled at her, "then, you'll be the wife of a police lieutenant."

"Oh, Mike for real? Did they promise you that? I'm so happy for you ... for us. Maybe, the kids will be gone long enough after all," she said, giving him a coquettish grin and tugging on his arm.

He pulled back, "No, let's wait till tonight. I don't want to rush. And besides, I've got to go out again."

With disappointment, "Go out ... where? I have supper ready, Mike."

"Put it in the oven, baby, I want to go and see Uncle Alcide, and you know if I don't catch him early, he'll either be in bed or stoned before long. I need him bad."

Her tone became sympathetic, "Poor man, going to waste, and with such a brilliant mind, too. Why did he retire from the force? They would have kept him on forever with his ability to solve crimes. Why do you want to see him? About the case?"

"Yeah, this is a complicated case. Hell, I'm not too proud to tell you I can use help on this one, but I wouldn't admit that to anyone else." He laughed, "Doesn't do my professional reputation any good to admit I need help on a tough case."

"It just proves you're human, honey. Takes a real man to admit he needs help sometimes."

"Yeah, I guess so, but, you see, this case is so important to me ... to us ... to the kids. It's a big chance for me."

She went to him, holding him close, "I know, honey, I understand. I'll put the supper in the oven. If you're leaving, I guess I'll go and pick up the kids so they'll be bathed and dressed for bed by the time you get home. You won't be too late will you? Want me to wait up ... just in case?" she teased.

"You bet," as he patted her rear on the way out.

Alcide J. Guilbert (pronounced in New Orleans Gee-BEAR), was his mother's brother. He had served in World War II, won a Purple Heart for

Summary Justice

his wounds and a Silver Star for his bravery, and had come out with enough time on the GI Bill to allow him to attend Loyola University to receive his degree in sociology. He naively believed that upon graduation if he applied his talents and his learning on the human race, he could make a difference, he could make the world a better place. He began as a teacher of sociology, trying to unravel the intricacies of the human mind, first in his students, then of society. The police department contracted his services more and more in their more difficult cases. Eventually, he migrated from a paid consultant to a permanent employee of the department and, eventually, one of the best investigative detectives in the nation. He never carried a gun. He hated guns in direct proportion to his hatred of violence. He, personally, never made an arrest. He left those matters to others. Like all the great detectives of old, he solved difficult cases with brainpower. His powers of reasoning and deduction were the stuff of legend, and he was often referred to as the "Sherlock Holmes of the New Orleans Police Department."

Now white haired, stooped with arthritis, and bitter and cynical with a human race he could not alter, he grew more bitter as he watched his beloved New Orleans become one of the murder capitals of the nation. He knew deep down in his heart that New Orleans was no worse than any other major city, but he took it personally because it was his town. He grew up in what was then the "Queen City" of the south. He remembered riding the streetcars up and down St. Charles and Carrollton Avenues, with the oak-lined sidewalks forming a shaded canopy and azaleas and camellias adding color any great artist would have been hard-pressed to duplicate, and then only in color, for the odor could not be duplicated.

He remembered his mother on those streetcar rides, as she sat there in her broad-brimmed straw hat (southern ladies avoided the sun like a plague) with white gloves, and, always, the parasol. Upon reaching Canal Street, she would exit with him, give him and his older brother each a quarter to go to the afternoon matinee at the Saenger or Loews State while she shopped. Now that world was gone, and that was why he was angry and cynical. Today, no mother in her right mind, he felt, would turn her young children loose on Canal Street and allow them to go to a movie on their own. That world was gone, he knew that, but ... why? That was what he did not understand. Why had society as he had known it, failed? He reasoned that it was due, as is most crimes, to socio-economic reasons, excluding crimes of passion. Since he could not change the system, he had resigned from it in disgust. His wife now dead from cancer, he lived alone in an old shotgun house not too far from the neighborhood in which he had grown up. Now he drank and smoked too much and bathed too little. He was aware of all his shortcomings, but as he often asked himself, "What does it matter?"

Mike saw his uncle's car in the driveway, so he knew he was in, unless he was taking his daily walk around the block, satisfied in the knowledge that he was exercising. He rang the doorbell, waited what seemed like a long time, then the door slowly opened. Alcide was scratching his head and rubbing his eyes as he saw his nephew, remarking, "Oh, it's you, Mike. What do you want?"

He smiled at his uncle, long used to his brusque manner, which only got worse as he got older. He patted the old man on the shoulder as he replied, "Good day to you, too, Uncle A.J."

The old man grumbled. "I thought I told you not to call me A.J."

Mike moved on in past him. "But, all your friends on the force called you A.J. Why can't I?"

"Because you're not one of my friends, you're my nephew. I can pick my friends, you were thrust upon me by a careless indiscretion of my sister and her husband," and he grinned as he added, "May her soul rest in peace. What do you want?"

"I need your help, Uncle."

"I don't have any money to lend you. Want a beer?" as he ambled to the couch and resumed watching the TV.

Mike felt as a public relations gesture to the old man he would accept a beer, replying, "Yeah, I'll get it. Want another one? I need to talk to you professionally."

The old man groaned in dissent. "Can't it wait? *Wheel of Fortune* is just about to come on. You know I win almost all the time. I could clean up if I went on that program." Accepting the beer from his nephew, "What do you want to talk to me about?"

"About the big case. They gave it to me today."

The old man grunted. "Congratulations, I guess. You should have fun on that one. Most interesting, most interesting."

He sipped on his beer, warming to the subject, "How'd you like to have fun with me, Unck?"

"Don't call me Unck, either."

Mike laughed. "What the hell do you want me to call you, then?"

"Nothing! I don't even want you to call me. Have Cindy call me once a week to see if I'm still alive. I like that girl, Mike...good woman...probably better than you deserve."

"Yeah, I guess you're right. I don't deserve her. At least, that's what she keeps telling me every night. Look, Uncle A.J., can we get down to business?"

"Yeah, I guess so. If I don't pay attention to you, you'll never leave, so ... " He turned the sound down on the TV, but he still watched the wheel spin. "What do you want of me?"

"I may need your help on the Gervais case. It means a lot to me," and he wisely added, "and to Cindy and the kids."

"Oh, yeah, why is that? What did they promise you if you cracked the case? Promotion to lieutenant?"

"Yeah, how did you know?"

"Figures! I know how they operate," and out of the corner of his eye, "buy an 'A' you dumb bastard; nothing else goes with that letter but an 'A'. Christ, people are dumb. So they promised you a promotion, huh?"

"Yeah, I need it bad, too. The boys are getting older and I want to send them to Jesuit, and that ain't free, you know."

The old man smiled. "You wouldn't be trying to use psychology on an old pro, would you, son?"

He shook his head. "No, I know better. Will you help?"

"I'm retired. The boys down at the station wouldn't appreciate an old war horse like me sticking his nose in their business, would they?"

"They'd never have to know. I could feed you the info here at home. All you'd have to do is what you have always done—use your head. All I ever saw you do was sit at your desk with your feet up, looking at the ceiling."

Alcide smiled. "Yes, but you see, I was working all the time," and he pointed to his head. "I let the gumshoes do all the road work and bring the info home to me. All I need is info to crack almost any case. Did you know that Sherlock Holmes hardly ever left his flat on Baker Street. Isn't that interesting? He let Dr. Watson run most of his errands."

Mike's eyes lit up. "That's what I mean. I'll run your errands for you. You just tell me what you want and I'll do it."

The old man turned off the TV set and looked up at the ceiling. "You know, it might be fun. I've been getting bored, lately. You know that widow who lived in the next block? Well, she moved to Dallas with her daughter. She was the only reason I took more than one bath a week, and now ... " he smiled. "I need something to get my mind off her. I was getting right fond of her. Damn good thing she moved. A man my age can get real silly over a woman, you know."

"Then, you'll help. My feet will be to the fire on this thing. City hall has got everybody stirred up on this."

He sneered. "Hell, they always do. I don't worry about them at city hall. I always told them to let me alone, or else ... "

"Yeah, you could get away with it, but I'd get fired."

"I suppose so. Let's get down to work, Mike. What do you people know about this case that I haven't read in the newspaper?"

"Not a hell of a lot. Let's have another beer and I'll tell you what we know, so far."

Surprisingly, he declined the beer, saying, "No, I need to keep my head clear, and so do you. Start talking," and he rose to get his pipe, filled it, struck an old-fashioned wood match to it, watched the blue smoke rise to the ceiling, and sat down, nodding towards his nephew.

Mike realized that the pipe was a catalyst to his thinking, just as it was to his mentor, Sherlock Holmes. It relaxed his body while nudging his brain into action. He gave his nephew a restless look, saying, "We don't have all night, you know. I want you out of here before the news comes on."

He cleared his throat, as he squirmed in his chair, moving to the edge of the seat. "Well, the known facts are just as the newspaper stated them: Marcel Gervais, New Orleans' leading architect, well known..."

"Hell, boy, don't waste my time telling me things we both already know. Let me talk to you for a while. Let me make some observations for you, simply based on what I know from the news media and some reasoning of my own. I knew Marcel Gervais, not well, but I knew him casually. He was a very handsome man. He could have been a movie star. Rich, successful, good family, big man in town. Smooth as silk. Could talk most men into things they really did not want to do, and I'm sure he talked a lot of women into things they really did want to do. He counted among his friends mayors, governors, senators, and just about every big businessman in town. He could have had most of the eligible women in New Orleans to play with, and quite a few of the non-eligible ones if he had just given them a hint he had wanted to, but he seems to have not been a promiscuous man. That is what makes this thing so interesting. Why would he fool around with this woman? Granted, she was a beauty, but they are as plentiful as leaves on an oak tree, and she was the well-known and often seen around town girlfriend of Jo-Jo Terrafina, son of the infamous alleged Mafia boss, Big Joe Terrafina. So, conventional wisdom would dictate that if a man was simply looking for a recreational roll in the hay, he could find a better and safer haystack than Miss Debra "Debee" Barre'? Incidentally, what do we know of her? Where does she come from. Did the police trace her yet?"

He shifted in his chair, really warming to the subject. "We don't have a lot of details yet, but she comes from down the bayou, below Raceland, down Bayou Lafourche; Golden Meadow, or Lockport—one of those small towns."

"No shit? How did she get from Bayou Lafourche to a hotel bed with the likes of Marcel Gervais? Wouldn't that make an interesting story, nephew?"

Summary Justice

"Well, we know some of it already. It seems she was a little beauty even in high school, cheerleader and all that. You know ... cream rises to the top kind of stuff. Well, she got some kind of scholarship, first to Nicholls State in Thibodaux, and she apparently soon outgrew that and headed for LSU in Baton Rouge. She appeared in some beauty contests and got her picture in the papers. She started going out with some rich kid in college and married him soon after. The marriage lasted only about two or three years and they were divorced."

The uncle scratched his chin, "Let's see, that would get her into her middle twenties, but she died at thirty-two. Where has she been the past few years and how did she get to be Jo-Jo's woman? There's about six or seven years missing in your travelogue of Miss Barre'. Jo-Jo goes through girlfriends like a man with a cold goes through Kleenex. They don't last long. She damn sure wasn't his girl for the past six or seven years. Where's she been? Find out."

He was making mental notes, hoping he could remember everything his uncle was saying. The old man got up to relight his pipe, going through the same ritual. Mike was sure it was part of his thinking process. He remained standing as he continued, "The hotel people—what do they know about this affair between Marcel Gervais and Miss Barre?"

"Mostly what the newspapers reported. They apparently met in the same suite every other Thursday at the same time for about two hours ... I suppose to have sex."

"Are we sure that is all they did ... have sex?"

He seemed surprised that his uncle would assume they were doing anything else in that suite. "What else would they be doing?"

The old man smirked. "That's one thing we need to know, Michael. Marcel Gervais was fifty-four years old. You, nephew, are only thirty-four years old. Do you need two hours to satisfy even your most elaborate cravings in that regard?"

Mike was genuinely embarrassed, but he replied with a mixture of shame and pride, "No, I don't need anywhere near that time. Maybe, he was a real stud."

"Ah-ha, that is something else we need to find out."

"For Christ's sake, how do you expect me to find out something like that?"

"Simple! You talk to his urologist."

Mike scoffed, "He'll never tell me something like that, you know, doctor-client privilege and all that."

"Michael, this is a murder investigation! You have the awesome power of the law on your side. Simply explain to him, or her, as the case may be, that you will get Mr. Gervais's records with his assistance or the assistance of a search warrant, and I know a judge friend of mine who will issue that to you without fail."

He made another mental note, "OK, I'll get the records, but suppose he has had no, you know, sex problems?"

The old man smiled. "Then, we can assume his prostate and his libido were both intact at the time of his demise. Speaking of his demise, I suppose the boys in blue have gone over the hotel room with a fine tooth comb. What'd they find?"

"Nothing of any value; no prints. It was done by a pro, I guess. Apparently, robbery was the motive because Gervais' money and credit cards were gone and the girl had no jewelry on her and she was well-known for wearing some large and expensive stuff." He watched the old man shaking his head as he concluded, "Why are you shaking your head, Unck?"

"Because, it was not robbery. No fool, even a crazy fool, will kill two people and risk the death penalty to obtain something he can acquire at the point of a gun. No, my boy, this is much more complicated than a simple robbery. What of the hotel guests at the time of the killing? Has the guest list been examined as yet?"

"No, that's the first thing I intend to do in the morning, but that will be a tough job. A big place like the Royal Orleans has hundreds of guests on any given day...."

"Don't waste your time perusing them all. Most people fit a profile, and you can eliminate ninety percent of them right off the bat. For instance, if a husband and wife checked in and checked out and they are from Lafayette, they probably are not involved, and if they checked in with a couple of kids, they damn sure are not involved. Get the picture. Concentrate on the lone males or females, especially where they went when they left. Bring me a guest list for that week. Come back tomorrow night at this time and I'll have a few pages of typewritten instructions and questions for you. I still have my old Underwood I used in my consulting days. Some keys are worn, but it'll do."

He rose to go, assuming the meeting was over. "Gee, Unck, I don't know how to thank you for helping me with this case."

The old man flicked on the TV set, and with a mischievous grin, "You don't think this will be a freebie, do you?"

"What do you want from me? I don't have any money, you know."

"How well I know, but you have a wife who can make a hell of a good pot of seafood gumbo. I expect some each and every week along with a six pack of Dixie."

He grinned. "It's a deal, Unck, but do I have to deliver, or will you come by in person to eat it with us?"

"Oh, hell, deliver it. If I agree to go to your house I'll just have to take a bath and it may not be time."

Mike looked into the old man's eyes as he said that. He had learned long ago that his uncle played with people and most of what he said was said tongue-in-cheek. He would watch to see what people's reaction would be to his outrageous remarks.

Mike persisted, "If you come to the house, you'll get to play with the boys. You don't get to see much of them these days. Why not?"

The old man grinned. "I would spend more time with the boys if you and Cindy had named at least one of them after me, but you didn't."

"Let's be honest, Unck. Would you want us to hang a Cajun name like Alcide on a kid in this day and time?"

"No! I guess not. Good night."

CHAPTER FOUR

The precinct station house was its usual morning madhouse of activity as Mike Fortier made his way to the cubicle which had been assigned to him as the head of the Gervais investigation. As he made his way through the secretary's area, he was beckoned by his office pal, Eve Edwards. He was her shoulder to cry on as she drifted from one ill-fated affair to another, believing each new one was "the real one."

"Mike," she practically whispered, "guess who is trying to get you on the phone?"

"The President of the United States?"

"Uh-uh, better than that ... Jo-Jo Terrafina. At least, his lawyer called for an appointment; says Jo-Jo wants to come in and talk to you."

Mike stopped by her desk. "Well, what d'ya know! I was going to pay him a visit today. Isn't that a hell of a coincidence! Get him on the line, Evie. And incidentally, how's the love life?"

She shrugged. "Don't ask. The last one is just like all the rest. He's only interested in one thing, and it ain't marriage."

"How did I guess that was the case," he teased as he walked by the desk of another detective. "Eddie. Get over to the Royal Orleans and get me a complete guest list of the week of the killing, OK?"

"Already did it. Here it is."

"Good boy. Now check the airlines and bus station for departures for that time."

"Will do, Mike."

"Mike, the attorney for Jo-Jo, a Mr. Salvatore Pataci is on the line," said the secretary. "Figures, huh," she laughed.

He picked up the receiver, "Sergeant Mike Fortier here, Mr. Pataci, may I help you?"

"Yes, good morning, Sergeant. I represent the interest of the Terrafina family, and my client, Mr. Jo-Jo Terrafina, feels sure you will want to question him in the Gervais-Barre' case, and he feels that he would prefer coming in on his own, since he has nothing to hide. Of course, I will be present during the entire questioning. Is that agreeable to you?"

Mike smiled into the receiver. "I wouldn't have it any other way, Mr. Pataci," and looking at his calendar, "Would ten this morning be agreeable to you?"

"No, I'm sorry, but that is too soon. I have other commitments. Is 2:00pm all right with you?"

"Two pm will be just fine, Mr. Pataci."

He rang for the secretary. "Evie, come in a minute. I need you to make a bunch of calls for me." As she made notes, he gave her names and numbers of people to call for either appointments or information. His adrenaline was flowing as he got into the case. Two people he had to talk to were the widow, Elsbeth Gervais and the deceased's partner, Irving Stern. But discretion dictated that he wait until after the funeral. Debra Barre's body was transferred to a small funeral home in Raceland and Marcel Gervais's was being handled by Schoen's with internment to take place in the Metairie Cemetery. He hoped to make the funeral, just to observe. He had learned long ago that, in a strange way, funerals can be very educational.

He had reserved the large interrogation room for the meeting with Jo-Jo Terrafina and his attorney, not sure how large a contingent they would show up with. He had observed these sessions before with Mafia families, and one thing he had learned, they are well represented. He had asked his lieutenant if he had wanted to sit in on the meeting, and he had declined with, "Nah, just fill me in later. It'll be the usual Mafia bullshit, with the attorney trying to make you believe that Jo-Joe goes to communion each and every morning."

They were right on time. At precisely five minutes of 2:00, a delegation walked in, comprised of Salvatore Pataci, two assistants carrying large briefcases (with copies of the U.S. Constitution, he was sure), followed by little Jo-Jo, himself, complete with elevator shoes and a thousand-dollar suit, if he had ever seen one. The attorney was impressive, with a full head of silver hair, a Roman nose, and a good set of teeth. Mike thought to himself, "If I were in trouble, I would want a man like Salvatore Pataci representing me, too." Jo-Jo, on the other hand, was not impressive. Balding, with a pocked-marked face and a large nose, he looked like a nervous little man. The only time he really felt big was when surrounded by several bodyguards—big bodyguards. His eyes went about the room, and his mouth twitched. He didn't like police stations, a condition he inherited from his father, who had spent most of his young life in them, but, in his later years had gotten smart and sophisticated enough to avoid them. He was officially retired as a dealer in produce—at least, that was the name on the warehouse on St.

31

Claude Avenue that served as his headquarters in New Orleans.

Mike motioned Jo-Jo to a particular seat and the attorney took the adjoining chair. The attorney, accustomed to courtroom procedure, waited until all were seated, looking at the tape recorder. He said, smoothly, "Sergeant, I was not aware that this meeting would be taped. After all, Mr. Terrafina came in of his own accord..."

Mike looked at him with some amusement. He had expected the objection, but said, "Are you making an official objection, Mr. Pataci? If so, it is noted and recorded. This is standard procedure to ensure that we all have a record of what is said, that's all. It avoids misunderstandings."

The attorney smiled. "I understand. Of course, we reserve the right to answer, or not, depending on the question. I'm sure you understand that."

"That is your client's right, Mr. Pataci, and now, in accordance with the law, I'll read him that right."

Upon the completion of that, the attorney stated, "If you don't mind, Sergeant Fortier, I have an opening statement to make on behalf of my client."

Mike glanced toward Jo-Jo, who was looking at the floor, twitching his hands and licking his lips profusely. Mike nodded to the attorney.

"For the record, let it be noted that my client, Mr. Joseph Terrafina acknowledges that he was a very close friend of the deceased, Miss Debra Barre', known to him as DeeBee. No, they were more than friends, they were in love and intended to marry. He, that is, we, felt that he would, without question, be dragged into this unfortunate affair, and to prove his innocence and good intentions in solving this horrible crime, he decided to come in to lend whatever assistance he could to the police in order to bring these cold-blooded murderers to justice. Mr. Terrafina is extremely bereaved by her untimely demise, and plans to go into seclusion at his retreat in Jamaica after we have completed this business, if that is all right with you."

Trying with extreme difficulty to keep from laughing at the attorney's speech, especially since the elder Terrafina had at least seven unproved murders to his credit, Mike replied, "No, Mr. Pataci, that is not all right with me. Mr. Terrafina will remain in the city until this investigation is completed. Is that clear?"

The attorney looked at his client, "We will comply, of course, but under protest."

"Of course. May I ask your client some questions, now, Mr. Pataci?"

"Of course, but may I remind you we came in voluntarily."

"I understand. Mr. Terrafina, you say you and Miss Barre' were engaged to be married? Is that correct?"

He answered in a high voice, almost falsetto, "Yes, that's right. Ah loved deh girl," and he almost sobbed, if one listened closely.

"Had the date of the wedding been set?"

Jo-Jo looked at the attorney, who replied, "My client last saw Miss Barre' on Tuesday night of that week. They had dinner together. They always do, because she leaves the next morning, Wednesday, to visit her mother who is in a nursing home in Raceland. She does this twice a month, always on the same day, Wednesday, and she spends Wednesday night with her sister in Golden Meadow."

Mike's eyes went wide at the mention of this schedule, asking, "Did Miss Barre' keep this schedule always? Did she ever stray from the schedule at all?"

Once again, the attorney answered, "Not to my knowledge."

Mike was getting annoyed. "Mr. Pataci, do you think you could allow your client to answer my questions directly?"

The attorney looked at a nervous Jo-Jo, "Of course, ask away," he smiled.

"Mr. Terrafina, can you remember if Miss Barre' ever changed the schedule we just discussed?"

He shifted in his seat. "No. It hadda do with deh nursing home and her sister's schedule ... no always deh same."

"I see. How did Miss Barre' make a living, Mr. Terrafina? Did she work for you?"

Jo-Jo could not suppress a smile. "Wal sure, she woiked fer me, but she was mah woman, too. Ya know what Ah mean. When eva Ah wanted it, she ... "

The attorney cut in. "I'm sure that goes without saying, Jo-Jo, but that is not what Sergeant Fortier means, I'm sure. You see, Sergeant, Mr. Terrafina is the president of Coastal Produce, a rather large importing company, and Miss Barre' was his executive assistant. They worked closely together, as you might imagine. That is why her demise will be such a loss to the company as well as a tragic personal loss to him," to which Jo-Jo nodded, blinking his eyes, sniffing a little.

"How much was she paid for all these services?"

The attorney stiffened. "I don't think that is germane to the matter at hand, so we refuse to answer the question."

"Look, counselor, Miss Barre' walked around this town with a fortune in jewelry strapped to her body. Her income is very germane to the matter at hand. I don't give a damn where the money came from at this moment, but I do care how much she made."

The attorney shifted in his chair. "Well, she made twenty or twenty-five thousand a year ... "

"Oh, come on, counselor. That wouldn't pay the rent for that apartment she lived in. We've had people out there, already. We've seen it."

"Well, of course, the job had considerable perks. Mr. Terrafina is a very generous man. The apartment was paid for by the corporation, I do believe," as he glanced at Jo-Jo, who nodded, sheepishly.

Mike had to get to the most pertinent of questions. He could wait no longer. "Mr. Terrafina, did you know Mr. Gervais?"

Jo-Jo's eyes lit up. Here was a question he could easily and truthfully answer. "Geez, eva body in dis town knows Marcel Gervais. He was a wheel."

"No, that is not what I mean, Mr. Terrafina. Did you know Marcel Gervais personally?"

"No ... uh, uh. Ah neva met deh man...Ah swear."

Mike nodded. "Then, did you have any idea that your fiancée was meeting Marcel Gervais twice a month in a suite at the Royal Orleans to have sex with him?" He could see that Jo-Jo was deeply wounded by the question, and strangely enough, Mike believed that his hurt was genuine, as he replied. "No, Ah wish Ah knew deh answer to dat one. Dat broad swore to me she wasn't balling nobody else ... dat's deh troot."

Mike took a deep breath, feeling he would get nothing more at this time, so he concluded with, "Jo-Jo, do you have any idea who would want to kill those two people as they did?"

He looked down at the floor. "No, Ah swear on mah mama's grave. Ah wisht Ah knew. Ah'd kill deh bastard..."

The attorney jumped at those words, "I want those words stricken from the tape. My client said them in a moment of extreme distress under unrelenting questioning by you, Sergeant. I want them deleted. Do you hear?"

"The words stay on the tape, counselor. If your client is as innocent as you say he is, what's the problem?"

Jo-Jo jumped up, now unrestrained. "Ah mean it, Sal, Ah'll kill deh bastard ... Ah tole ya dat. Ah tole deh ole man deh same thing ..."

The attorney grabbed his client by the arm. "This meeting is over, Sergeant. Either charge him or get off his back."

Mike smiled. "That's all, Mr. Pataci. I appreciate your coming in with Mr. Terrafina."

He watched as the attorney and his client, along with the two ever silent assistant attorneys walk through the busy police day room, careful not to brush up against any of the mass of humanity which characterizes a typical day in a station. He smiled, thinking, I hope they didn't soil those silk suits.

"How'd it go?" asked Eve the secretary as he passed her desk. He sat down for a minute, smiling as he opined, "You know, Evie, this job is really a study in human nature. Would you believe that little bastard just about convinced me he actually loved that broad."

"There's just no explaining taste, is there? You know, come to think of it, since I'm between boyfriends just now, and Jo-Jo has just lost his girlfriend, maybe he and I can become a twosome, huh? He *is* loaded with money, isn't he?"

He patted her cheek, "Aw, you can do a lot better than Jo-Jo, honey. You're a real dish."

She touched his hand for just a brief moment. "Careful boy, you're getting awfully close to sexual harassment in the workplace." As he withdrew his hand, she exclaimed, "Geez, I hate that feminist movement. Give me the good old days when I got propositioned at least five times a day." She yelled after him as he walked off smiling, "Sometimes ten times on a good day ... I swear!"

He parked his unmarked police car a long way from the other mourners' cars at the funeral of Marcel Gervais in Metairie Cemetery. He looked up at the clear blue springtime sky, thinking, "It's a good day for a funeral." He looked around, perusing the crowd. It was just as he had expected—a lot of important people were there. He could see the mayor and city council standing next to the lieutenant-governor, and then he saw the immediate family—Elsbeth Cartier Gervais and her two daughters. It was easy to pick out the widow. Hardly a day went by that she was not seen in the newspaper or on the evening news, connected with some charity or organization or something. She was quite an activist and her two daughters were following in her footsteps. The oldest, Andrea, about twenty-five, was married to an attorney. She was attractive, but no beauty. But the youngest, Victoria, now there was a beauty. About twenty-two and still single. She had gotten the best features of her two handsome parents and the results had been stunning. As patricians, all three were bearing their respective grief in silence. They were the kind of people, he felt, who do their crying in private, keep their emotions in check in public. Not too far from the Gervais family he could see the business partner, Irving Stern and his wife.

He moved closer to the bier area, trying to be as unobtrusive as possible. As he stood not too far from the Gervais family mausoleum, constructed of pink granite with white marble angels embossed in bas-relief, he grunted, "Geez, that place cost ten times what my house cost, I bet." Glancing to the west, into the bright sun, he watched a large black limousine park on one of the side access streets. Curious, he moved closer for a better look. Two men in dark suits emerged and extracted a large funeral wreath from the jump seat area of the limo and proceeded to the general area where many wreaths were piled one on the other. Mike moved in closer, close enough to be able to read the large card tied to the wreath with a red ribbon. It read: WITH SYMPATHY ... TERRAFINA FAMILY. Mike stared in disbelief. Why would Jo-Jo Terrafina send flowers to the funeral of a man who was shot balling his girlfriend? Unless, it were just a P.R. gesture to convey the impression that there were no hard feelings. Clumsy attempt he felt, but then, Jo-Jo was not famous for class or finesse.

Mike stayed only a short while longer and then, feeling he could not accomplish anymore, he, too, backed away and made his way to his car. It had been a long and trying day and he knew he would have a long session with his uncle that evening, so he concluded, "I'm going home to play with my two boys."

Cindy looked at her husband as he finished a meal of liver and grits, mashed potatoes, green salad, and a beer. She laughed as she poked him in the ribs. "There's nothing wrong with your appetite, Sergeant Fortier, believe me. You must have a hell of a metabolism to absorb all those calories and not get fat. Gosh, you men are lucky. Everything we females eat ends up right here," as she patted her buttocks.

"Yeah," he responded, "that's where you girls need padding to absorb all the punishment you get there."

"Yeah, punishment inflicted by the male of the species, and the babies you give us. Men!"

"What would *you* do without *us*?" He rose. "I hate to end this cerebral discussion but I've got to go to see my old uncle. I've got be sure I can see him between *Wheel of Fortune* and *Bonanza* reruns or it agitates him a great deal."

"It doesn't take much to do that, nowadays, does it?"

"Oh, I guess it's a lot of things. First, the death of Aunt Cecelia, and then, no children of their own, then, he's growing old. Between the arthritis and the hemorrhoids, he is either aching or itching."

She laughed. "Are you trying to be funny?"

"Yea. Well, I got to go."

Embracing him, she asked, "Will you be late? The kids like you to say goodnight, you know."

"I know. I'll be home before then. Bye."

As Mike rang the doorbell, he looked about the front porch. The shotgun house was typical of New Orleans of the early part of the century, with its three or four rooms in a row. Usually, part of one room had been sacrificed to make way for a bath in later years. The porch had the usual four lathe-turned cypress columns, long devoid of paint and now a patina gray in color. The yard was recently cut and the walks were trimmed, showing the old man still cared about appearances, if not his own. He came to the door, saying, "Oh, I figured it was you. Good thing the *Wheel* just ended or I wouldn't let you in."

"I know. I timed it that way."

"You're learning. Come on in. We have a lot to cover before *Bonanza* comes on. Did you get the information I asked you to get?"

"Yeah, including the hotel guest list. But first, let me relate my meeting this afternoon with little Jo-Jo and his attorneys."

"That should be interesting, but you can forget about Jo-Jo, he didn't do it."

"I agree, but what makes you so sure."

"It's not his style. Mafia killings are not that finessed. They catch some poor guy in front of a saloon and blow him to bits, or they make sure the body disappears, like to the bottom of the river, or in Jimmy Hoffa's case, who knows where? What have you got?"

"First, let me tell you of the meeting with Jo-Jo." As he related the entire conversation, the old man went through his pipe lighting ritual, saying from time to time... "Uh, huh...mmm'mmm...," and then, "Like I said, he didn't do it. This was a professional hit job, but that is what makes it so perplexing. How would Marcel Gervais get involved with anything that would make him the victim of a professional hit job? That's the puzzle, my boy, and that's what we've got to find out."

"Isn't it always sex or money?"

"No, not with the Mafia or their types. There are things that mean more to them than that, although money is the ultimate fuel that drives the machine. Sex is easy to come by. Money is a lot harder. Don't forget the Mafia kills for something as simple as who gets to work this side of the street or that one; in other words, territory."

"Would Marcel Gervais ever get involved with the Mafia?"

"I didn't say he did. I'm just saying it was a professional hit job, very clean. Now, let's see the guest list. Get us two beers as I go over it, and that's the only one tonight for both of us."

As he walked to the kitchen he said, "You were right, Unck, I went over the list while I ate my liver and grits, and you can throw out over ninety percent of the list right away. I had one of my assistants red line the obvious throw always, so it will save you some time..."

"Let me decide that," he replied. As he accepted the beer he grumbled, "Don't sit there doing nothing while I review the list. Here are my twelve typewritten pages of questions and procedures for you to look into. Starting tomorrow, I want you to get busy interviewing Mrs. Gervais and the partner, Mr. Stern. The next day, you and I are going down the road to Bayou Lafourche."

He looked up surprised. "I thought you told me you didn't want to get personally involved—publicly, that is."

"I did say it and I meant it ... here in New Orleans. I'm too well-known in police circles and it could hurt you. It might make you look like you can't solve this case on your own and that would hurt your career. If you lost your job, then I would have to support you, your wife, and your kids ... get it?"

Mike looked for the tongue-in-cheek grin and, gratefully, he saw it as he asked, "What will we do in Bayou Lafourche, as if I didn't know."

He smiled. "I'm going to eat some good catfish, that's what. They know how to cook catfish down there," and as he continued his perusal of the list, he said, "The trouble with most restaurants that serve catfish is they really don't know how to cook it. I like my catfish well done. I hate to have that damn white milk come out of it when I eat it."

Not really interested, but in an effort to humor the old man, Mike asked, "And how do you avoid that?"

"Well, it is really quite simple. First, the deep-fry oil has to be 375 degrees—no more, no less."

"Why is that so critical?"

"If the oil is cooler than that, the meat will absorb the oil and it will end up greasy. If hotter than that, the fish will overcook on the exterior and the inside will be undercooked and milky."

He grinned. "So, that is the secret to good catfish, huh?"

"No, that's only half of it. Cut the filets into small pieces, nuggets they call them now, dip them in a good Cajun batter, and fry them for four or five minutes, then," and he rolled his eyes towards heaven, "if God had made anything better, he would have kept it for Himself."

Mike shook his head. "The things I don't learn from you, Unck."

"I told you not to call me Unck! OK, I went over the list. I've narrowed it down to seven or eight people I want you to run down. I see that this fellow, Emile Rashid, never checked out of the hotel according to this note. Find out why. Have you had time to run over my list?"

"No. I was learning to cook catfish ... "

"If you're going to walk with me, you had better learn how to walk and chew gum at the same time. Take the list home and study it. Now, go home and see your wife and kids. My hemorrhoids are bothering me. I want to be alone for a while."

Mike looked to see if he was smiling. He was not, so he replied, "OK, I'll see you tomorrow night to let you know how I made out with Mrs. Gervais and Irving Stern."

He nodded. "Mike, go easy with Mrs. Gervais. You're dealing with a lady, not one of your precinct hookers."

"Yeah, I know. I'll remember. Goodnight."

After seeing the kids to bed, Mike returned to the small living room where his wife was watching TV. She smiled as he fell into a lounge chair, closing his eyes in fatigue. She went over to him and began to massage his shoulders, "Tired, sweetheart? Good thing I caught you last night, huh?"

"Yeah, good thing! This case is enough to wear me down. Most cases are physical cases, you know, some punk kills a tourist in the quarter, takes his money and credit cards, and then proceeds to make every mistake in the book, and we have him in twenty-four hours or less. It does not take a genius to solve those cases. That's why I call them physical—no brain work; but this baby is different. You know, if some conventioneer or some traveling salesman had been killed in that suite, with that woman, it would be a lot simpler, but Marcel Gervais? Geez!"

"Do you think it was all about sex?"

"No, it's more complicated than that."

"H'mmm, I don't know. You men sometimes do crazy things for the want of one particular woman. Frankly, I never quite understood it."

He grinned at her. "Well, honey, you see, it's simply a matter of testosterone."

"Maybe, you should all go to the vet for a cure, if you know what I mean ... "

He looked up at her. "Does that include those two boys I just put to bed? You know, your two sons?"

She smiled. "Certainly not! I want grandchildren," then she kissed him on the forehead. "But, you will solve it, I know. I have faith in you. I'm going to bed. Coming?"

He looked to see if she had that look in her eye. She didn't, so he replied, "No, I want to think this thing out for a while."

She assumed a worried look. "Honey, you're not going to let this case get you down, are you?"

"No, I promise it won't, especially if old Uncle Alcide holds out. Don't forget, you owe him a pot of seafood gumbo this weekend."

She stopped. "Oh, yeah, I forgot. Will you peel the shrimp?"

"Sure."

"Are you going to devein them?"

"No, it adds to the flavor."

"Oh, you're disgusting. If you don't devein them, I'm not making the darn stuff and you will be in hot water with your uncle."

Lloyd J. Guillory

"You, too."

"Uh-uh, he likes me. You told me so."

He blew her a kiss. "Women! Go to bed."

He leaned his head back on the lounge headrest and mentally went over the entire case. "There has to be a crack somewhere. There always is, and once the daylight comes through that crack, the whole thing comes into view, but ... where is the crack?"

At his house, Alcide J. Guilbert stared at the ceiling. "One little opening, that's all; then, it's like a crowbar. You insert it and wham—it breaks open."

In the large mansion on St. Charles Avenue a bereaved widow climbed the stairs to her bedroom ... it had been their bedroom. She sat at her dressing table, her glance moving from her reflection in the mirror to the silver framed photo of her late husband, only this day lowered into his grave ... gone forever. The tears previously held in check, now began to flow easily. She was alone. This was the time to cry. In the mirror she could see the bed, their bed, where so many expressions of love and passion had taken place. She sobbed as she asked, "Why, Marcel? Did I fail you? If so, how? Was I inadequate in my later years, or, was it just a midlife crisis fling? I would have forgiven you, you know, if only you had come to me and explained it. I would have forgiven you." She lowered her head on the marble top and allowed her grief to flow, unebbed, her hands clenched in despair and grief.

Down the bayou, in a small town, a woman sat on her bed and stared at the photo of her sister who had made it "big." She sobbed as she ran her hand over the photo of her loved one who had also been lowered into her grave that same day. "Oh, Debbie, if only you had stayed here with us. We could have lived without the extra money."

CHAPTER FIVE

He was surprised that Mrs. Elsbeth Gervais had agreed to see him on Sunday morning, the day after the funeral, but as she had explained it over the phone, "Let us get this unpleasant experience over with. You will have to wait until I get home from church. We ... I ... always go to 10:00am mass, and if you will allow me time to get home from church, I'll be willing to see you. Shall we say 11:30am?"

He had always admired the beautiful home whose yard comprised almost an entire block along St. Charles Avenue, where real estate did not come cheap. He remembered his uncle's admonition with regard to Mrs. Gervais, "You're dealing with a lady, not one of your precinct hookers." He had lain awake several hours the night before, going over the questions he would ask and the tone with which he would ask them. He knew he would have to get personal, and he hated that. He would be forced to ask her questions no one had ever asked her before in her entire patrician life, but he had to.

The dependable Martha answered his ring, after hearing from her mistress, "That is probably the police sergeant, Martha. Please show him into the library," and to her daughter, Victoria, "Come along dear. I would like to have you sit with me through this ordeal."

Martha had a deep rooted and inherent distaste for anyone even remotely connected with the police due to awful memories of police brutality to the members of her race when she was a young girl. She opened the door cautiously, as if she expected some harm to come to her. He cheerfully said, "Good morning. I'm Sergeant Fortier of the NOPD. Mrs. Gervais is expecting me," he smiled.

"Yassuh, she waitin'. Come in, please," and she gave him a wide berth as if he had a contagious disease. She pointed to the library. "She waitin' in deh liberry. You kin go right in."

He saw Elsbeth Gervais and her daughter, Victoria, sharing the same couch, as if to give moral support to each other. He attempted his best smile as he went forward to meet them. Victoria stood, but her mother did not, instead extending her hand, saying, "Good morning, Sergeant ... Fortier, is it not? A good old French name. This is my daughter, Victoria. I've asked her to join me in this meeting. I hope you have no objection to that."

He could see both women had swollen eyes from many hours of shedding tears. He replied, "No, Ma'am, that will be fine," and he shook the daughter's offered hand.

Ever the gracious hostess, even under these conditions, she asked, "May I offer you some coffee, Sergeant? And, perhaps, some cookies. We have not eaten anything this morning, as yet, since I receive communion every Sunday. Are you Catholic, by any chance?" As he nodded, she continued, "Even though we are allowed to eat before Communion these days, I guess I'm still old fashioned. I refrain from doing so until ... but I'm beginning to chatter, aren't I? Please go on," as she handed him a serving tray of coffee and cookies. He could not help but admire the china and the silver service.

"Mrs. Gervais, please accept my apologies for having to bother you at all, but I'm sure you understand that I, we, the police have a duty to do."

She slowly sipped her coffee, attempting a smile at her daughter as she responded, "I know, as unpleasant as all this is, that certain formalities must be followed. We, the family, want to know the answers too. We must," she added as she discreetly dabbed her eyes with a tissue. Her daughter patted her hand, saying nothing, as the mother continued, "Have they arrested him yet?"

He looked perplexed. "Arrested who, Ma'am?"

She stiffened. "Why, that horrible person who obviously perpetrated this crime, that Jo-Jo Terrafina, who else?" He noticed that the daughter nodded in agreement, also dabbing her swollen eyes.

He seemed embarrassed to respond. "No, Ma'am, we have not arrested Mr. Terrafina. We have questioned him, but he is not a suspect, as yet ... "

She cut him off, "Why, that is absurd! Who else could have done it? I'm not quite sure, Sergeant, just what my husband was doing consorting with the likes of a ... a woman like that, but there is little doubt in my mind that it was an act of vengeance, pure and simple," she sobbed.

It was the daughter who spoke up next, "Surely, you're not going to tell us that someone else might have done this?"

He nodded, looking from one to the other, "Yes, even though we have no hard evidence to support this theory, that is exactly what we believe." He felt more comfortable with the plural, "we", since his more experienced uncle believed that also. He watched the two women gasp as they

Summary Justice

sunk down in their seats, breathless. They both asked in unison, "But who? Why?"

"We don't know that. I'd like you both to think hard about that. Can you think of anyone Mr. Gervais knew or did business with who might hate" ... he regretted the word he had used, so he changed it to, "To have been so upset or unhappy with him that they could do this?"

It was the widow who insisted, "But, the girl? Isn't it rather conclusive, as distasteful as it appears, that this was a crime of," and she shook her head, for the word pained her ... "a crime of passion?"

"It would appear so, at first glance, but Mrs. Gervais, it is too complicated for that."

"Complicated? It seems rather open and shut to me! Someone shot them and robbed them. Is it more complicated than that?"

"Yes, Ma'am, we think so."

Her hands went to her throat, as she turned to her daughter, also staring in disbelief, as she exclaimed, "Oh, my God! What is that all about? What is happening to our lives?"

He sighed. "That is what I'm trying to find out, Ma'am. Did your husband have any business worries, you know, financial problems?"

She shrugged and managed a smile, waving a hand around the magnificent paneled library, and then the other hand all around, as she replied, "Really, Sergeant, does it look like we have financial problems?"

"No, Ma'am, not any immediate financial problems. I meant big financial problems—in his business, for example? Maybe problems involving huge amounts of money?"

She seemed offended. "What on earth are you implying? Why, my husband is noted for integrity and honesty! His professional reputation demanded that. He handled large amounts of his client's money. He had to be above reproach," she insisted.

"I know, Ma'am. I'm not even attempting to insinuate anything to the contrary. I'm just trying to piece this together. Solving a crime is a lot like putting a jigsaw puzzle together. One piece leads to another ... "

"Well, I suggest you look elsewhere than at the integrity of Marcel Gervais," she said proudly, with Victoria nodding in agreement.

"I meant no offense, Ma'am," and continuing, "Were you very familiar with all your husband's business affairs?"

She poured him and herself more coffee, with the daughter shaking her head. "No, thank you, Mother". She responded, "No, not in recent years. You see, Sergeant, it is generally well-known in business circles that my family's fortune exceeds my husband's by a considerable amount. I administered my family's money and he administered his own." She seemed embarrassed to be discussing personal finances with a complete stranger, but felt the situation demanded it. "Our money was actually handled separately. We shared household expenses and things like that, but other than that ... " and she shook her head.

"Then, it is possible that your husband could have had business activities you knew nothing about."

"Well, of course, but what are you getting at?"

"I'm not sure, Ma'am, I'm just looking at all possibilities," and turning to the daughter, "Miss Gervais, I need to talk to your mother alone. Would you mind?"

She turned to her mother for directions, with the mother replying with a shrug of the shoulders. "You run along, dear. I'll be perfectly all right," as she patted Victoria on the hand.

The daughter rose to go. "Are you sure, Mother?"

She nodded, motioning, "Yes, run along."

"Well, all right," she responded with some concern, "I'll be in my room if you need me."

The mother managed a smile. "I'll be fine. Would you ask Martha to bring in some hot coffee. More cookies, Sergeant?"

He replied, "No, thank you, just coffee," and as he watched the library doors close behind the daughter, he turned to the mother, "Mrs. Gervais, I have to ask you some personal questions that I felt sure you did not want your daughter to hear."

She stiffened. "Any questions you did not want my daughter to hear are probably too personal for you to ask me," she replied with indignation.

"Probably, Ma'am, but I need to ask them anyway."

She removed a handkerchief from a purse, dabbed at her eyes, and proceeded to twist it, nervously, adding, "Go ahead, let us get this over with. I reserve the right to refuse to answer any question I deem improper. I am not a suspect in my husband's death, am I?"

He seemed offended that she had asked. "No, Ma'am, of course not, but we feel you want to see justice done in this matter."

She nodded. "Why do I feel that it will be poetic justice? Please get on with this; I have a full afternoon planned."

He looked down at the floor, clearing his throat. "Mrs. Gervais, did you and your husband have a satisfactory sex life?"

He could see her face stiffen as she replied, "What is a satisfactory sex life, Sergeant? Can you define it?"

"No, Ma'am. The experts tell us that whatever a couple is satisfied with ... for them, that's all that counts."

"Then, using that definition, my husband and I had a satisfactory sex life, and I am grateful you had the good sense to ask my daughter to leave. Thank you."

Summary Justice

"Did you have any reason to believe that your husband was having an extramarital affair?"

She sniffed. "Certainly not! If I had, I would have confronted him with it. My husband and I had been married nearly thirty years. I regarded him as a completely faithful husband all those years. I can't explain this situation, this tawdry affair, except to classify it as a mid-life crisis of some sort." Then, with consternation, "Is this a private conversation, or will this show up some day in a written report for all the world to see?"

"No, Ma'am, it is as private as I can make it. You will notice that I am taking no notes. Everything you are telling me will be left with me, alone."

"Thank you, I appreciate that. Is there anything else?"

"Just a few more questions, Ma'am. Did you and Mr. Gervais share the same bedroom?"

She seemed truly offended at that. "Really, don't you think you are getting a little too personal? Next thing, you'll want to know how often we had sex."

"Yes, Ma'am, that's my next question."

"That's absurd! I refuse to answer such an insulting question. That has no bearing in this case."

He sighed. "That's what I'm trying to find out, Mrs. Gervais. Was your husband's liaison with this woman a sexual thing or not?"

She stared at the floor for a long time, obviously thinking the whole line of questioning through. Shaking her head in obvious embarrassment, she quietly said, "Sergeant, I am fifty-two years old. I am post-menopausal. Do you understand what that is to a woman and what it does to her?"

He nodded. "Yes, Ma'am, I had a mother."

She looked out the window. "My husband and I had separate bedrooms. He is a very light sleeper and he wakes up all hours of the night and reads a great deal, sometimes for hours at a time. I, on the other hand, require my eight hours or more of sleep a night, so we decided on separate bedrooms several years ago. It is no indication of any dilution of our love and devotion to one another; simply a civilized way of solving a very minor sleep problem, that's all. I would hardly offer that as an excuse for his unfaithfulness. My husband was not sexually deprived, if that is the thrust of your argument. As a matter of fact," and she paused to consider her statement, "I have myself wondered what that woman could do for him that I couldn't. I'm sure every wife who has been betrayed by her husband has asked the same question." She looked him coldly in the eye. "Now, Sergeant, I think, this meeting has gone on long enough. You now know as much as my confessor, with less justification, since you are not able to save my soul." She rose, motioning him to the library door, and taking him by the arm. "Sergeant, I need to know what this is all about. Do you need any help with this thing? More police support, for example? I am not without some influence at city hall, you know."

"No, thank you, Ma'am, I have all the help I need," and he mentally thought of Alcide J. Guilbert. As they reached the front door of the house, she looked him in the eye, and placing a hand on his arm, "Please solve this thing. I have to know."

He nodded. "Yes, Ma'am, I intend to."

As he drove away from the Gervais mansion, he yawned, knowing it would be a long day. He had awakened early, trying not to disturb his still sleeping wife, who had promised him that she and the two boys would accompany him to 8:00am mass at Loyola on St. Charles, with the wifely admonition, "At least, Mike, if you *have* to work on Sunday, let us try to maintain some semblance of family life by going to church together, as a family." He could not argue with her logic. Actually, he seldom argued with anything Cindy said to him, for he had discovered his loyal and loving wife was usually right. It was she who provided the stability in their marriage, he knew that. He had married a "good girl" as his departed mother used to remind him. He hated having to conduct these meetings on a Sunday, but the captain had promised him two weeks off when, and if, he cracked this case.

"Two weeks, Fortier, for you and the missus to go anywhere and do anything you want, if you crack this baby in short time." He retorted with, "But, what is a short time, Captain?" to which the senior officer replied, "Any time that will get the Mayor off the Commissioner's ass and him off mine—that is short time, Fortier!"

And now, with the widow's questioning out of the way, he had only Irving Stern, Marcel Gervais's partner, left for the afternoon. He drove home to a Sunday dinner with the wife and kids. He felt sure the dinner and the reception would be cold, but the kids met him with their usual exuberance, each asking, obviously in previously arranged unison, "Can we go to Audubon Park when you get home this afternoon? Can we? Huh?" From one, "I want to see the animals." From the other, "I want to ride on the train."

He laughed. "Yes, if I get home early enough, we'll go to the park. Where's you mama?" and then from the kitchen, "I'm in here, Mike, trying to keep the dinner warm."

He poked his head in the doorway. "Sorry, I'm late, honey. I thought I'd get through with Mrs. Gervais in thirty minutes, but it took a while longer."

Summary Justice

Cindy, coming up to him for a quick lip brushing kiss, said, "Was she able to tell you anything?"

"Aw, you know honey, I never tell you anything about my police work."

"Aw, B.S., Mike. Did she know anything?"

He smiled, "No, poor soul. She didn't know what was going on. You know the old saying. 'The wife is the last to know.'"

Cindy gave him a cold look. "I hope this wife will never be put to that test."

He held her close. "No, baby, you know better than that. What's for dinner?"

Returning to the stove, "Cold chicken, cold potato salad, cold bread," and looking back at him, "but, a warm-hearted cook."

He gave her an appreciative grin. "That's all that counts, honey."

As he sat at the table and she began to serve the food. "Have the boys eaten?"

"Yes, you know how they are when mealtime comes. I asked them to wait for you, but I wasn't sure when you would come home, so after fifteen minutes of complaining, I fed them. Do you mind? But I waited for you."

"That's all that counts. What would I do without you?"

"Probably not as well", then, plaintively, "Honey, do you know what time you'll get back from talking with Mr. Stern?"

"I'm not sure. Why?"

"Well, heck, Mike, it's Sunday. I want to do something—go somewhere—see something."

He nodded. "I understand that. Why don't you take the boys and visit your folks while I'm at Mr. Stern's. When I get through with him, I'll call your folks to see if you're still there."

She shook her head. "No, I wish I could. Have you forgotten that promise you made to your uncle?"

"What promise?"

She grunted, "The promise of a supper of seafood gumbo each and every week. Remember? I have to stay home and make it, and you have not peeled the shrimp or ... "

"Oh, honey, I'm sorry! I've been so damn preoccupied with this case."

"Don't worry about it, Mike. You go play policeman and I will do my job. Isn't that what it's all about it?"

"I'm sorry I really am, but, I swear when I get home we'll do something."

"What?"

47

"Anything you want, honey."

She sighed, "The boys want to go to the park. Didn't I just hear you promise to take them after work?"

He sucked his teeth. "Yeah, I did."

She laughed. "Then, I guess that is what we'll do, and in the meantime, I'll make gumbo. Now, go on about your business."

Irving Stern lived in a raised cottage house, just off Fountainbleau Drive, in a nice neighborhood. It did not compare with the pretentious mansion of his late partner, Marcel Gervais, but he and his wife, Olga, were happy there. They were not pretentious people, believing instead that a house was not one of the world's best investments, but merely a tool for living. Their children now grown and gone, they lived for each other, and their bond grew stronger with each passing season. It was for this reason that Irving Stern had insisted that she be present during the interview, telling her, "No, my dear, this traumatic event will touch our lives most assuredly, and we will face it together, as we have all other crises in our marriage." She smiled and patted his hand.

Since the Sterns had no servants in house, certainly not on Sunday, it was Olga Stern who answered Mike Fortier's ring. She smiled a warm smile as she asked, "Yes?" in a cautions tone, not knowing for sure if it were he.

He displayed his identification credentials. "Mrs. Stern? I'm Sergeant Mike Fortier of the NOPD. I believe Mr. Stern is expecting me."

She nodded. "Yes, he is. Please come in. Lovely day, isn't it? It's a shame you have to be working today."

"And a shame that I'm forcing you to do the same, Ma'am."

"Oh, we don't mind. My husband and I do a lot of reading on Sunday afternoon until the heat of the day passes, and then we go out for a walk, so you're not bothering us one bit. Here is my husband. He was in his basement workshop, playing with his toy train." She smiled as she saw him coming, adding, "It's his main hobby."

Irving Stern approached, not smiling, for he smiled seldom, and he viewed this interview with distaste, telling his wife only that morning, "What can he ask me? I know nothing of that woman and Marcel's relationship with her. I only had suspicions, Olga," to which she replied, "Irving, merely answer his questions, darling." Mike had known Irving Stern only from occasional photos in the newspapers and on TV when one of their larger projects was in the news. Irving disliked being on public display at any time, leaving those chores to his more gregarious and, most certainly more handsome partner, Marcel Gervais, who loved the limelight. Mike sized him up: a man in his mid-fifties, short of stature, bald, with thick eye glasses, and in a rumpled jump suit with grease stains on the chest.

Irving Stern managed a weak smile, saying, "Please forgive my appearance, Sergeant, I've been playing with my trains and I sprayed some WD-40 on my chest. I had allowed myself some time to clean before you came, but," and he chuckled, "when I get started with my trains, I forget all about the time."

Olga laughed. "He is worse than a little boy where those trains are concerned. You should see that layout. May I offer you some coffee, Sergeant?"

He shook his head. "No, Ma'am, thank you. I just got up from the dinner table. My wife cooked one of my favorites—chicken stew and potato salad."

The couple smiled in unison, with the husband asking, "Would you like to see my train layout? Some people tell me it is quite impressive, although I have been playing with it so long, I can't appreciate it as much as a stranger."

He hated to think of wasting time looking at a model train layout, remembering his promise to his wife and children, but he felt he could not refuse the man, so intent was he about the invitation. Mike replied, "Why, yes, sir, I'd like to see it."

With apparent delight, Stern replied, "Come on down these stairs; be careful, they're narrow. The layout is in the basement." (The typical New Orleans "raised cottage" design was a derivative of the old plantation homes which had been raised one story in height above the low ground elevations of south Louisiana for several very practical purposes: to get the main floor safe from floods, to allow some air to circulate under the house in the damp coastal climate, and to afford some protection from wild animals and insects. As the area developed in later years and flood protection measures were instituted, the raised floor was enclosed by most homeowners and the above ground basement developed into usable living space.)

As he came out of the stairwell and entered the huge space formed by the basement with only supporting piers dividing it into smaller modular units, Mike gasped in disbelief. He saw a wonderland of tracks, scaled model villages, hills, rivers, and bridges. Irving Stern had combined the love of his hobby and his engineering genius for design and construction to produce a wonderland of make believe. He stood by, proudly, as he waved his hand in a circling motion. "This is it. You're looking at my 'mistress', as my wife calls it. She complains that, at my age, I would probably spend less time with a real woman than I do with all this, and," he chuckled, "she would see more of me."

Lloyd J. Guillory

Mike smiled. "Do you think she means that, Mr. Stern?"

He returned the grin. "No, I don't think she does."

Mike walked around the room, amazed at the size and complexity of the layout. He gazed from one direction to another, shaking his head in disbelief. Irving Stern walked to his master control panel, fully computerized, beckoning the policeman to come forward. He proudly pointed to the master control board, exclaiming, "I can control each and every segment of this layout from here. I can even program it to do what I want, when I want," and saying that, he began to push buttons. The sound of water was heard everywhere. Mike's eyes widened like a child's as rivers began to flow, waterfalls began to drop their flow over rocky precipices, mill wheels began to turn as they did over a hundred years ago. He stood there, shaking his head in wonderment as Stern stood there like a symphony conductor bringing to life and sound each portion of a major symphonic orchestra as he pushed buttons off and on. Mike watched his face, filled with rapturous pleasure at his creation came to life, and then, either tiring of it, or feeling that his guest was, he began to push buttons which brought it all to its natural state of inactivity. He gave Mike a weak smile, saying, "I don't want to bore you anymore with my childish pleasures, but all men have some weakness, do they not? Some men hunt and fish all the time, some chase women, some gamble, some are sport nuts. Me? I play with trains," and pointing to the door, "shall we go back to the world of reality?"

Mike took one more look at the world of fantasy, and then, with great hesitation, "Mr. Stern, would you mind if I brought my two boys out here someday to see all of this?"

"Not at all! I'd love to show it to them. This is to me like a great painting or a fine piece of sculpture in somebody's closet. What good is it if no one sees it."

Olga was waiting for them when they returned to the living room, smiling, sitting before a pot of coffee and cups. She pointed to a chair, saying, "I know you said you were not in the mood for coffee, but I thought after that exhausting train ride, you might have changed your mind."

He smiled, nodding. "You're right, too. I have changed it. That model train layout is incredible. I've never seen anything like it. It should be in a public place where everyone can enjoy it."

Irving Stern smiled. "It will be, after I'm gone. Now, Sergeant, can we get down to the unpleasant business at hand. I don't relish this anymore than you do, but I guess it must be done. What a tragedy. What a tragedy ..."

Mike Fortier realized that he liked these two people. Although he had never met Marcel Gervais, he was sure this couple was warmer, more human, more compassionate than the Gervaises. Perhaps, he thought, you can overbreed gentility into people, like a thoroughbred race horse or a racing greyhound—they're always nervous and on edge. He preferred calmer people who had less gentility and more compassion, less pretension and more warmth.

Irving Stern was mild mannered, patient, and at peace with himself, but still disturbed by the new trauma in his life. He waited until the policeman had finished his coffee, and with some nervous hesitation said, "Well, Sergeant, I guess it is time to get to the matter at hand, as unwelcomed as I feel that it is. I don't feel that I know anything that will be of interest to you in your investigation, but I am willing to help if I can." He looked at his wife who smiled faintly at him and patted his arm as if to lend support. He placed his cup on the coffee table, leaned back on the couch, and with hands extended, "Ask away."

He extracted a notebook from his coat pocket, saying, "I hope you won't mind if I take notes. This case is getting a little bit complicated and I have to resort to writing some of it down."

The engineer looked a little surprised. "Complicated? I thought it was an open and shut case, Sergeant. Marcel was foolish and careless enough to fool around," and he gave his wife an apologetic look as he continued, "and he was killed by a jealous boyfriend. Is there more?"

"Yes sir, I think there is. Mr. Stern, did you know of any problems that Marcel Gervais might have had, you know, not personal problems, but business ones?"

"As you might suspect, Marcel and I led completely different lives, not only because of our different religious backgrounds, but simply because we were completely different kinds of people. Mrs. Stern and I," and he looked lovingly at his wife, "did not mix with the Gervais family to any great extent. We made marvelous business partners, I think, because of that difference in lifestyles. The Gervaises seemed to love the lime light, the parties, the socials, that sort of thing. Olga and I preferred our home and our grandchildren in our spare time. As you know, Marcel was an architect and I am an engineer, and I suppose those two different disciplines also led to our divergent lifestyles. Architects, at least those I know, are more gregarious, more outgoing, than my compatriots and I seem to be."

"Then," asked the policeman, "other than seeing each other in the office, you and Mr. Gervais seldom saw each other out of the office?"

He nodded. "That is correct. Even in the office, which is divided into two components, he ran the architectural office and I ran the engineering office. Our respective fathers, who founded the firm, did pretty much the same thing."

"But, there were some projects on which architecture and engineering were involved, were they not?"

"Oh, of course! Many of them."

"Were any of your projects in trouble? Especially, any major one, involving large sums of money?"

He furrowed his brows. "I'm not sure I know what you mean. I don't know how much you know about the design business, but we don't fund our projects. They are funded by the owners, whoever they might be, public or private. We work on a fixed-fee basis on almost all projects. We have been a very successful firm for over half a century, and the firm is in very good shape financially, I can assure you." He smiled, as he looked at his wife. "The Gervais men, even Marcel's father before him, felt that we Jewish boys could handle money better than the Cajuns," and he chuckled, "so they always let us be in charge of the finances. Marcel used to stick his head in my office door, asking in a joking way, 'Irving, do we have any money in the bank?'"

"So, we can assume the firm had no money problems?"

He shook his head. "No, we are financially solid, including our employee retirement plan. It is fully funded and invested in blue chip stocks."

"Can you think of any project you had in the office that could present a financial problem?"

He shifted in his chair. "Well, the only one that could even remotely fall in that category, and I believe that has been straightened out, is the Esperante Project."

The sergeant looked interested, "Could you tell me what that is all about?"

"Well, as you know, Louisiana has passed a riverboat gambling bill, as have so many other states," he said, "some without much of a waterfront, actually, and the bill has been kicked around in the legislature and the city council and who knows where it will all end."

"Then, the Esperante Project has to do with a gambling casino?"

He looked up. "Oh, much more than that. The entire project was of considerable size because it was to include not only the gambling boat, or craft of some kind, but a theme park, a major hotel, and more—quite a project. Actually, one of the largest we have ever had in the office."

"Tell me about it, please."

"I really don't know much about it, because it is only in the design phase and the engineering has not come into the picture as yet. Besides, Marcel handled this one. It was his baby."

Summary Justice

The sergeant was definitely interested. "Surely, a project of that size could not be kept secret. Where was it to be built?"

He shrugged. "That was one of the problems. Poor Marcel; it seemed that no matter where he tried to locate it, he ran into some very stiff environmental opposition from several quarters ... "

He interrupted, "But, you gave me the impression that those problems would have belonged to the owners. Why did Marcel Gervais get involved in that?"

Irving Stern gave his wife a nervous look. "Well, you see, this was one project that Marcel had more than a designing interest in. He was to be one of the partners. As a matter of fact, it was a limited partnership type of entity, and he was the general partner."

The policeman, not being well grounded in finance, asked, "What is a limited partnership?"

"Well, in a limited partnership, the general partner pretty well runs the show and the limited partners, mostly investors, are just what the term implies, they have a very limited role. The everyday administration of the project is done by the general partner."

"And that was Marcel Gervais?"

"In this particular case, yes."

"Then, let me get this straight. Marcel Gervais would have been one of the principal owners, and the firm of Gervais and Stern would have been working for him and his partners. Is that a fair evaluation?"

"Precisely, Sergeant."

"How large was the project ... in dollars, I mean?"

He sighed. "Well, the final budget had not been established because the design was only in a preliminary stage, but Marcel told me one day that we were looking at some fifty million dollars worth of work in the firm," and then he added, "at least."

The sergeant, who had never had the pleasure of dealing with anything larger than his house mortgage, whistled. "That is a lot of money. Where did the financing come from? Did you ever bother to ask Mr. Gervais about that?"

He smiled. "Yes, as a matter of fact I did. You should know, Sergeant, that when a Jewish boy hears about that kind of money, he takes an interest in where it comes from, especially so when you realize that, even if we end up with a ten percent fee, which would be fairly close, we're talking about a five million dollar fee for the firm. Yes, I did ask him and he said the financing was all arranged with some large Canadian bank. I don't remember the name, but I know they have already financed one or two large office buildings in this city, and they knew of us because we designed them. Lenders take a hard look at the track record and solvency of its design teams."

Mrs. Stern stood up, straightening her skirt, asking, "Are you sure I can't get you gentlemen some more coffee? This looks like it might be a long session."

Both men nodded, with the sergeant resuming the questioning. "Then, we can assume that the project was funded?"

The engineer assumed a sheepish look. "Well, I had been informed that it had, but just recently, Marcel mentioned something about the Canadians getting scary because of the environmental problems. It seemed they wanted no part of that and he, Marcel, mentioned something about some other financing."

"Did you have any idea what came of that?"

"No. Marcel handled it all, because you see in his role of the owner, he did not have to explain that to me. It was an unusual situation for the firm to be in, you know, wearing two hats."

"This sounds like a lot of trouble. Why would Marcel Gervais take on all that responsibility? He didn't need the money, did he?"

"Oh, personally, I don't think so, especially if you include Elsbeth's ... Mrs. Gervais's money ... have you met her yet? She is quite wealthy in her own right, but they keep their money separate," and his hands went to his mouth, as he added, quite sheepishly, "I really had no business telling you that. I hope that will not go into your notebook."

The policeman smiled. "If it will make you feel any better, Mrs. Gervais has already told me that, but to get back to my question, why would he want to go through all this trouble, all this environmental crap ... oh, excuse me. Mr. Stern, sometimes my precinct language gets into my genteel conversation."

The older man smiled. "I use the word myself," and he looked around to see his wife returning with the coffee, "when my wife is not around."

"What are you talking about, Irving, that you can't say in my presence?"

He grinned a mischievous grin. "I was just telling the sergeant that I never use the word "crap" in your presence, my dear."

She smiled. "But, you just did, Irving," and she began to pour the coffee, adding, "I'll leave you two men alone," and made a gracious exit after bidding the policeman good day.

The husband watched her leave, with obvious affection, as he grinned and said, "It's a wonder she didn't say 'You men will be better able to express yourselves if I am not here.' That's what she generally says," he smiled.

Not to be deterred, the sergeant persisted. "I asked you to tell me, if

Summary Justice

you can, why Marcel Gervais went to all this trouble with this project. As a big city leader, he could ill afford to run afoul of the environmentalists on this thing. Is that not correct?"

"You are quite correct. I asked him the same question, but you see I already knew the answer."

"Can you tell me?"

The engineer sat back in his chair and looked down at the floor. There was no doubt he was reluctant to talk about the matter, but he started slowly. "Well, I was hoping we would not have to get into this because I can't see how this had anything to do with what we're discussing. There is nothing specific that he told me ... it's just something that one man can perceive for himself, especially when it concerns someone he works with each day," He took a deep sip of the cup, mulling the words over in his mind, wondering how to explain it without hurting the memory of a fine man. He leaned forward in his chair. "You see, Sergeant, architects have egos larger than their works justify, some worse than others. Frank Lloyd Wright was a case in point, but in his case, he was one of the few who had a talent larger than even his ego. Marcel Gervais was a very talented architect. His buildings and his works lend a lasting testament to that talent, but he peaked out some twenty years ago. Oh, don't misunderstand me—he didn't lose his talent, he just couldn't stomach the turn of the profession when it left what is generally mislabeled 'modern' architecture. That is generally referred to as the style practiced by Wright, Neutra, Saarinen, and others. When the next movement came in, which is generously referred to as 'post modern', he could not stomach it. It was that style he referred to as 'crap,' and he would add, 'pure, unmitigated crap.' Of course, the firm had to do it to keep in touch, but more and more, Marcel let the younger men and women in the firm handle it, and he did more sailing and played more golf. He became somewhat bitter about a profession that had 'left him' as he put it, sometimes adding, 'turning to the left.' He was especially bitter because he knew he could not change it. It took even a giant like Wright a half century to see the profession change. Why, the AIA didn't even honor the old man with their coveted gold medal until he was ready to die. And do you know what he said as he got to the podium at the award ceremony? 'Well, it's about time!'"

The engineer looked at the younger man. "Am I boring you with all this irrelevant information?" and not waiting for an answer, continued, "It's the only way I can explain about the Esperante Project. You asked why would he go to all that trouble? Well, as I saw it, this was his last chance to make a big splash, the kind he was used to making years back, when his beautiful designs were on the evening news and in the newspapers the next day."

"I don't understand what you mean, Mr. Stern."

He sipped his coffee, arranging his thoughts. "Remember, I told you he was both owner and architect on this project. As general partner, no one had the legal clout to tell him to change his design ... he would be in control of a massive project and he could design it the way Marcel Gervais wanted to. That's how I see it. It was to be his last hurrah, as they say, and he would have done anything to bring it to fruition." Stern became pensive as he added, "I'm not sure, however, that he would have been willing to give what he did give—his life."

The sergeant shifted in his chair. He was anxious to bring this talk to a close. He remembered the promise to his wife and kids. He pressed on. "Mr. Stern, can you think of anyway this project could have degenerated into, what it did?"

"My God, No! What has the project to do with him being in that hotel room with that woman?" he asked, his voice rising in honest incredulity.

"I don't know, Mr. Stern, but I damn sure intend to find out."

"I sincerely hope you do, Sergeant, although I'm afraid none of us will like the answer."

"That's a possibility, sir." Rising, he added, "Mr. Stern, I can't thank you enough for spending this time with me on a Sunday afternoon, and I am grateful for the train trip, too," he joked.

"My pleasure, Sergeant, and don't forget to bring those boys of yours around to see it, too."

"You can bet on that. Please tell Mrs. Stern good-bye for me, and good day to you, sir. Thanks again."

As he returned to his car, he looked at his watch. Four o'clock! If he hurried home, he could keep his promise to his wife and children by taking them to Audubon Park. As he drove north on Fontainblieu, heading for Carrollton, he mulled over Irving Stern's conversation. He was now more confused than ever about the circumstances of Marcel Gervais's death. "What the hell was he doing in that hotel room with Debra "Deebee" Barre'? Was there a connection?" He couldn't see it. He could hardly wait to inform the uncle of his talk with the partner. Perhaps, the older and more experienced investigator might see some light.

His sojourn to Audubon Park fulfilled as promised, and with the two sweaty boys in the bathtub, he walked to the kitchen with his wife. He opened the fridge. "Want a beer, Cindy?"

At the stove, stirring a pot of shrimp okra gumbo, she replied, "No, thanks. I'll drink one with the meal. I have to get ready for Uncle Alcide." She smiled, shaking her head, "Gee, I hope he's in a good mood. He is so much fun when he is, but when he's moody, well ... " and she stirred the pot.

At six sharp, the doorbell rang. "Honey," she yelled over the TV, "that's Uncle Alcide. Would you get it?"

"Got it," he grunted. Cracking the door an inch or two he joked, "We gave at the office!"

He expected some sarcastic comment in return, but, instead, "Those azaleas could stand some watering, Mike," and moved on in, brushing him as he did. Mike sniffed the air. "Come in, Unck. You smell like a precinct hooker. What is that I smell?"

He turned to him, proudly. "Faberge ... BRUT. Women are crazy about it. Besides, it's better than that musk crap you use. You smell like a billy goat all the time."

Mike had not had the opportunity to take a good look at his uncle, but as he did, his jaw dropped. His hair had been cut, the silver reflecting in the light. His trousers had a crease in them and he was wearing a coat and tie, both fashionable. The nephew was impressed. "Gee, Unck, you didn't have to dress up just for us."

He interrupted. "I didn't. I did it for Cindy, not *us*! Where is she?" and he headed for the kitchen, asking, "Where is my Dixie beer? That was part of the bargain, too, you know. Damn that gumbo smells good. Where are the boys?"

Cindy looked up from her cooking, sweaty beads of perspiration on her brow. He took her in his arms and kissed her on each cheek, saying with a grin, "Damn, I love women; especially when they're sweating."

"Oh, Uncle Alcide, you always catch me at my worse. You didn't give me time to freshen up, but, I'm glad to see you anyway. How are you? We don't see enough of you."

He grinned as he popped his Dixie. "Well, you will, honey, every weekend until his debt is paid off."

She gasped. "*His* debt? What does he have to do with paying it off? I'm doing all the work. Can't you see that?"

He took a deep swig on the beer. "I know, my dear. I've already thought about the inequity in this arrangement. That's why I'm taking you to Las Vegas when this is all over, just you and me."

She grinned at her husband. "Is that all right with you, Mike?"

He grinned back. "Sure, if a man can't trust his uncle, who can he trust?"

Alcide went to the stove, opening the lid on each pot. Tasting the brew, "You should really have put more pepper in that gumbo, Cindy."

"I know, but the boys have to eat it, too, and they can't take all that pepper."

He smiled a mischievous smile. "Can't we send them to McDonald's?"

"I thought you liked to be around the boys."

"Not if they're going to interfere with my gumbo," he teased.

She smiled. "I never know whether to take you seriously or not."

He patted her shoulder. "I'll let you know when I'm serious, Cindy. Until then, you can assume I'm kidding. Where do you want me to sit?"

"Oh, anywhere you want to. Mike, will you get those boys to come and eat. I thought they were hungry."

Seeing his nephew go through the door, the uncle asked, "Is my nephew treating you all right, honey?"

She seemed surprised at his concern. "Of course, Uncle Alcide, he treats me fine. Why do you ask?"

He shook his head. "No special reason. I just wanted to be sure. You know I'm fond of you ... and Mike, too. You're all the family I have since I lost my wife. We don't have much of a family, do we?"

She gave him a warm smile, patting his arm. "You know we are always here, if and when you need us."

As he patted her arm in return, the boisterous boys burst into the room, jockeying for their place at the table, pushing and shoving. Their father, after seeing a frown on the face of the uncle, grabbed both youngsters by the scruff of the neck, saying, "OK, you two, you can leave the room and come back in a civilized fashion, or, you can go to bed hungry—take your choice!"

He could see a smile on the uncle's face as the chastised boys made a new entry. Mike grinned. "Let's eat, folks."

Later, Cindy served coffee in the small living room as the two men settled down for an evening session of "braining," as the uncle called it. Having finished with the coffee, she looked at both men. "If you gentlemen have no further need of me, I think I'll get these boys to bed, and then I guess I'll go to bed and read." She grinned. "If we had a large house, you could go to the library and I could go to the drawing room ... "

Alcide rose to tell his niece goodnight, asking, "Would you be any happier in a larger house?"

"No. I'm happy in my little shotgun house. I was just teasing my husband. He knows better." She kissed her husband on the cheek, asking, "Should I wait up for you?"

He gave his uncle an embarrassed look as he replied, "No. We may be late. We have a lot to cover."

Hearing the phone ring, he said, "You get that, will you, honey?"

The two men sat facing each other, each taking a tablet off the coffee table, as Cindy yelled from the hall where the phone was located, "Mike, it's a Mr. Stern. He says he needs to add something to the conversation you two had this afternoon. Can you take it?"

"You bet. S'cuse me, Unck. Want more coffee? Help yourself."

Watching his wife disappear into their bedroom, Mike picked up the receiver. "Hello, Mr. Stern. Mike Fortier here."

"I apologize for calling you at home, Sergeant, but I remembered something after you left that I probably should have brought up."

"Oh, really, well, I don't mind your calling me at home any time you need to. What is it?"

"Well, in going over any projects that you think might have some bearing on this case—you know—troubled projects, I forgot to mention one that might have some bearing. I guess I forgot it because it has nothing to do with architecture."

"Oh, what is that?"

"Well, it is an oil well drilling venture Marcel became involved with, and from what he told me in brief conversations, it has turned sour ... from a financial situation."

"What happened? Do you know?"

"No, I don't. He never gave me details, but I remember he used to get some upset whenever he mentioned the thing, to the point of cussing all the other partners. That's all I know, really. I'm not sure this is even relevant to the matter at hand."

"Mr. Stern, at this stage of the game, everything is relevant until we decide what is not. Does this venture have a name?"

There was silence at the other end for a moment, then, "Let me think for a moment ... yes ... I remember he mentioned it. It was called Tradewind Drilling, or something like that. He also used to mention a man named Grover Canton. I feel sure that is it."

"Anything else?"

"No, that's all. Probably will amount to nothing, but I just felt you should know."

"I appreciate your call. Goodnight, Mr. Stern."

Returning to his uncle, he related the call to him. The older man furrowed his brow as he looked up. "Grover Canton, huh?"

"Yeah, the name mean anything to you?"

"Not much. He is a con artist; always coming up with some get rich quick scheme. I read about him the last time he was in trouble with the law. Some of his partners had filed suit against him for selling some mineral leases too many times to the same parties."

"Do you think we have anything pertinent there?"

The uncle scratched his head. "I don't know, but it is worth looking into. But, for now, let's go over the Stern meeting. Tell me what he had to say."

The nephew related as best he could each and every detail of the meeting with the engineer, glancing from time to time at his notebook, ending with, "And you ought to see that model train layout; it's fabulous. I can't wait to take the boys out there."

The uncle didn't answer for a long time, obviously deep in thought. Finally, "Mike, this thing is beginning to take on an odor of its own ... this Marcel Gervais thing."

"How do you mean?"

"It is becoming clearer and clearer to me that Marcel Gervais was involved in some things he had no business being in. Not a man of his caliber, anyway. I can buy Irving Stern's explanation of his partner's unusual participation in the gambling boat project ... this Esperante Project, for I knew Gervais well enough, especially by reputation, to know that he had a big ego, an ego which was not being fulfilled as of late. He was also a man in mid-life, a terrible time for men who go through a menopause of the mind, so to speak. I remember my own when I was foolish enough to ... but I digress. What puzzles me, though, is the oil drilling venture, if Irving Stern had it right. We have to check it out, for sure."

"I'll put some people on it in the morning."

The uncle interjected. "Have you forgotten that we are supposed to go to Bayou Lafourche in the morning?"

"No, I haven't forgotten. I'll get up bright and early and go to the precinct office. I'll make a tape giving instructions to the secretary as to what I want from all my assistants the captain has given me, and then, I'll pick you up at your house and we'll head down the bayou, OK?"

The old man looked at his watch. "In that case, I'm ready to go home. I need my sleep, considering I get precious little even when I am in bed. Nine o'clock, shall we say?"

Mike nodded at him, hands raised in questioning. "Are we making any headway, Unck?"

The old man halted, squinting his eyes. "I think so, though we are a long way from cracking it. We need a break, but let's see where we are. Marcel Gervais, who up until now has led an ordered existence, even according to his own wife and partner. Then, all of a sudden, he is killed in a hotel room with a Mafia cutie, and he has made some business departures he generally didn't make. That is all we have, Michael, my boy. Perhaps, tomorrow, we can get some inkling of how Debra Barre' fits into all this mess. One thing for sure, she is no innocent bystander."

"You don't think so?"

He rose to go. "No, I don't think so. This isn't about sex, I'm sure of that. Oh, I don't deny the sex thing is too obvious to ignore, but, it is more involved than that. And," as he paused at the door, "I've been meaning to ask. Did you call the credit card company to find out if anyone used Gervais's gold cards? I understand from the newspaper account that his office said he carried two gold cards, Visa and Master Card, each with a twenty-five thousand dollar credit limit. They have been canceled by now, I'm sure, but did anyone use them in the past three days since the killing? Have your office check on that, will you? In the meantime, I'll bet you ten bucks that no one used the cards. Wanna bet?"

"No, Unck, no bet! I learned long ago not to bet against you and your hunches."

He smiled. "That's a good thing. Now, go to your wife and kids. Leave the braining to me; gives me something to do. I was beginning to atrophy," and as he went down the steps, he called back, "damn, that gumbo was good. Thank Cindy. Tell her your debt is half paid. This thing won't go another week."

CHAPTER SIX

As Mike pulled his car to the curb in front of his uncle's house, he could see the old man sitting on the porch, smoking his pipe. He could further see that, once again his uncle was immaculately dressed, replete with tie and jacket, and even more surprisingly, a colorful handkerchief in his jacket pocket.

As the uncle walked up to the car he could be heard whistling a tune whose melody was not recognizable to Mike but he smiled at the uncle. "You seem happy this morning, Inspector Clouseau," he teased.

"Laugh if you will, my boy, but on a day like today, I have a new lease on life. Some excitement has come into my mundane life," as he lowered his body into his nephew's car.

"You mean the Gervais case has renewed your interest in life and given you a reason to carry on?"

"Nonsense! The case has nothing to do with it." He smiled, "When I got home last night I had a message on my machine from Rosalie. She's coming back to New Orleans. Seems the move to Dallas with the daughter didn't work out or, as conventional wisdom might conclude, she found she couldn't live without me."

He grinned at the old man, not knowing if he were serious or not. "But, Unck, that means bathing even when you don't need one ... "

He put his smelly pipe in his jacket pocket after shaking it out the car window, replying, "And worth each drop of water and grain of soap, but enough about romance, let's get down to business. The credit cards—did you have time to check on them?"

"Yes, I had a man do it, but you were right, there have been no charges since the day of the murder, and now they have been canceled by the family."

"Just as I thought, Michael. This was no ordinary robbery. This was a professional killing. The killer was just having fun with the police, that's all."

"But, a professional killing would mean that some very big people were displeased enough with one or both of them to have them blasted away."

As he slid down in the seat, relaxing, "Both of them to be sure. He did not have to kill them both if he had not wanted to. He could have picked either of them, anytime and anywhere. They were not heavily guarded people. No, my boy, they offended someone," and he added as he closed his eyes, "seriously offended them."

"Would you prefer that I take the Huey Long bridge or the Luling One?"

"The Luling One, of course. It's much shorter to Boutte and Highway 90, is it not?"

The old man dozed off and he could be heard snoring and on some occasions, snorting. The nephew smiled as he took occasional glances at his mother's brother. Since his mother and his uncle had no siblings, and he, Mike, had none, the old man was most of his "family". The old man stirred as Mike swerved off U.S. 90 and took the exit to LA 1, the road down Bayou Lafourche to Grand Isle, Louisiana's only claim to a sandy beachfront. He sat up. "Where are we?"

"We just turned on LA 1 and heading down the bayou. Where did they ever get a funny name like Lafourche ... do you know?"

"Oh, Michael, how unfortunate that your mother, my late sister ... may her soul rest in peace," and he crossed himself, "did not allow you to speak the tongue of your ancestors in her home. If she had, you would be a more erudite man than you are, and you would know, without my having to tell you, that Bayou Lafourche comes from the French word for fork, and that is "fourchette.""

He shrugged his shoulders. "But, why name a bayou after a fork?"

"Because, you miserably uninformed creature, Bayou Lafourche was at one time a major fork of the mighty Mississippi."

He was surprised. "I didn't know that."

The old man snickered. "Add that to the myriad of other things you don't know. For your edification, the Mississippi has had four major changes of course at its outlet into the gulf. The Lafourche one peaked out about 1300 AD, forming this ridge on which we are now riding."

"Where do you learn all this?"

"Reading, Michael, reading. But enough about geology. Did you find out if Debra Barre' had any more siblings besides the sister we are going to visit?"

"From what we learned, there were two girls and a boy, with the boy being much older than the girls, because the mother married twice. The boy was killed in Vietnam, so we were told. That leaves just the surviving sister now that Debra is gone."

"When was Debra buried?"

"Saturday, the same day as Marcel Gervais."

"Where was she buried?"

"In Golden Meadow."

"Did you send someone to observe the funeral?"

He gave the uncle a sideways glance. "You know I did. I sent one of my best men."

"Was Jo-Jo present at the funeral? After all, he professed his love for the woman to you, did he not?"

"Yes, he did, but I guess his love did not run that deep after all. He was absent, but he did send a hell of a big wreath, though."

"How touching. Does the sister know we're coming?"

"Yes, I called her. I forgot to tell you this, but she asked something strange when I identified myself as New Orleans policeman. She asked, 'Are you going to arrest me?' and she added, 'I have to know because I have four children at home, and I would have to make arrangements with someone to take care of them. My husband is a shrimper and he is out most of the time.'"

"That is most interesting! What did you say to that?"

"Well, I had to tell her the truth. First, I explained to her that I would be out of my jurisdiction and could not arrest her if I wanted to, and, secondly, I told her that I was not aware of any reason to arrest her."

The old man shifted in his seat, bothered by his arthritic hip. He looked out the window, muttering, "That is interesting, very interesting. I feel our visit with Mrs. ... what is her name?"

"Mrs. Martin ... Nedra Martin."

"Ah, yes ... Mrs. Martin. I feel this will be a very interesting visit." The old man rolled down the window, sniffing deeply at the incoming air. "God, I love to smell that odor of seafood. It makes my gastric juices begin to flow. I can taste that fried catfish already," and he smacked his lips, adding, "Do you know how to find that sister's house?"

"Yes, she gave me rather detailed instructions. It seems it is out in the country, about two miles before we get to Golden Meadow."

"Then, how will you find it? Do you know where to turn off?"

"More or less. It's the third house after the Texaco station, right after the volunteer fire station, so keep your eyes open for the fire station, first."

"OK. Oh look, there's a seafood diner. We'll have to keep that in mind on the way back, and over there, I'll bet that's the fire station. They always fly the flag. Yes, that's it. You're home free, now. There's the Texaco station, too."

Summary Justice

The name on the rural mail box listed Martin, Nedra and Oscar. The house was set back from the road about a hundred yards, as were most houses along that one street area. The yard was surrounded by a barbed-wire fence. The entrance road was blacktopped, not shelled as were most of the others. At first glance, the house was not very impressive, but as they got a closer look, they could see a rather imposing addition had been added to the rear, as if to hide it from the public, or as the uncle commented, "The assessor."

A very nervous woman answered their ring. She looked as though she had been very pretty at one time, but now, whether through negligence or disinterest, the bloom was off the rose. She had combed her hair, not stylishly by any means, and her dress was the kind she might have worn to church on Sunday. A cross of embossed silver hung from her neck. She attempted a smile as she opened the screened door. "Come in please. I guess you're the policeman who called me from New Orleans," she asked with trepidation.

Mike Fortier showed her his ID, replying, "Yes, Ma'am, I'm Sergeant Michael Fortier of the NOPD, and this is my uncle, Alcide Guilbert," adding, "he came along for the ride and to get some Bayou Lafourche fried catfish."

She wrung her hands in nervous agitation. It was obvious to both men that she was not relishing this talk, as she led them through the front parlor, toward the rear of the house. They finally got to the newer addition, a very impressive family room, complete with a large masonry fireplace and cypress woodwork. It was a pleasant room, well appointed, and no doubt cost more than the original house. The two men looked around, noticing a hallway that led off the family room, so the addition was larger than they first thought. She motioned them to chairs, saying, "I noticed you both have Cajun names so I guess you're coffee drinkers," adding, "I'll bring it in. It's on the stove. I make real drip coffee, so it might be a little strong for you."

The old uncle smiled. "No, Ma'am, that's the kind I like, although my nephew might like some milk in his. He is only half Cajun," he joked.

The coffee having been served and drunk, the woman sat twisting her hands in her lap. Her eyes, too, were swollen from crying over the loss of her only sibling. Mike exchanged glances with his uncle, then, "Mrs. Martin, I really do appreciate your taking the time to see us, and my uncle and I want to express our deepest sympathy over the loss of your sister. It is not our intent to add to your misery, but simply to get some facts which might aid us in solving this unfortunate tragedy."

The uncle smiled at him, thinking, he is getting good. I could not have made a better introduction, myself.

Lloyd J. Guillory

The nephew continued. "As I told you over the phone, this is not my jurisdiction. I have no authority here in Lafourche Parish, so you don't even have to talk to me if you don't want to, but, I hope you will."

She sniffed. "Oh, I want to find out who did this as much as anyone else. I loved Debbie so much. We were as close as two sisters could be." She dabbed at her eyes with a tissue. "I know she had her faults, but she was kind and gentle. She would not have hurt anyone. I don't understand why anyone would have wanted to hurt her." She pointed around the room. "She gave us all this. We would not have this room if it hadn't been for her. She was so generous."

The two men gave each other sideways glances, as the nephew continued. "Mrs. Martin, how much did you know about Debra's work? Did she talk about it very much?"

She shook her head. "No, not too much. I know she worked for a company named Coastal Produce, that's all. She must have made good money because she helped us out a lot. She drove a nice car and she wore expensive clothing, I know that. I was so happy to see her make good, especially after her marriage broke up. She married too young. They didn't know what life was all about," and she looked embarrassed as she added, "I think she married him for his money. That's always a mistake, isn't it," she asked.

"You're referring to her first marriage, right out of college?" the sergeant asked.

The woman nodded. "That was her only marriage. I couldn't understand why she never married again ... so beautiful, so smart. I used to ask her, 'Debbie, why don't you find yourself a nice man and get married?' She always had the same answer. 'Nedra, if I ever find a nice man, I will.'" The woman sniffed, wiping her eyes. "And I guess when she did find the right man, she couldn't have him."

The sergeant asked with reservations, "I suppose you're referring to Jo-Jo Terrafina, her boss?"

The woman could not suppress a smile. "Oh, God, no. She didn't love him. He loved her, but she certainly did not love him. She told me that in no uncertain terms. No, she fell in love with an older man. She would never tell me his name, only that he was a big man in New Orleans, and that he was married. She told me he told her he would never leave his wife but she continued to see him. I guess, now, we all know who that man was. I tried to warn her 'Debbie, don't get involved with a married man; it will just end in misery for you,' but," she shrugged, "you know how love works. She should have stayed in Miami where she lived for a few years. Maybe, she'd still be alive."

Both men's eyes widened noticeably at the mention of Miami. It was the older man who could not suppress his interest, saying, "Forgive me, Mrs. Martin, for intruding into the conversation, but I'm a retired policeman and I'm helping my nephew in this very difficult case." She nodded in agreement as he continued, "Could you tell us all you know about her years in Miami?"

She sighed and shrugged. "Well, when her marriage broke up, she was so disgusted with this part of the country, she just wanted to get away. She was beautiful, you know, oh so beautiful, and smart, too. Well, she bought an airline ticket to Miami to visit a girl she knew from college. She got a job in Florida and in time she did real well, I guess. She'd fly home to see me every six months or so, and she began to send me money to help out." She looked embarrassed. "My husband is a shrimper, and you know how that is—when they catch a lot of shrimp, the price goes down, and when they don't catch much, the price is high. Either way, you barely make a living at it, and now the government has come out with all those new rules about turtles. My husband says if he knew how to do anything else, he'd quit shrimping."

Mike asked, "And your mother, she is in a nursing home in Raceland, is she not?"

The woman nodded, then shaking her head, "That's where Debbie's extra money came in handy. I don't know what we would have done with Mama if we didn't have the money to keep her there. I guess she'd be on public welfare, or something, because I couldn't help her on my husband's income. I have four children to raise and educate ... it's so hard these days."

The uncle persisted. "What did Debra do in Florida? Do you know?"

She shook her head, raising her hands. "No, she just told me she was the executive assistant to some man and he paid her well. I know she did a lot of traveling for him. I'd get cards from all over the Caribbean and South America all the time. Oh, how that girl traveled."

The two men exchanged glances, with the uncle asking, "But, you have no idea what she did for him?"

She gave both men an embarrassed look, twisting her hands, then, plaintively, "I guess I may as well tell you the whole story. What difference does it make now that she's dead. She was in love with a man in Florida and he was crazy about her. He wanted to marry Debbie, in the worst way, but she just wouldn't do it—marry him, I mean."

"Why not? Did she tell you?"

She sat, shaking her head. "Yes, he was in the rackets some kind of way, from what I understand. She wouldn't tell me anything more than that, even when I questioned her."

"If she was in love," Mike asked, "why did she leave Florida? Do you know?"

"To get away from him. When she made up her mind not to marry him, she felt she had to go on with her life, so she moved to New Orleans." She raised her hands. "I'm not sure that move was an improvement in retrospect."

The uncle asked, "Would you happen to know the name of the man in Florida?"

"Yes, his name was LaRoca. Gino LaRoca."

Mike exchanged glances with his uncle, who had raised his eyebrows at the mention of the name. Feeling he could get nothing more from the Miami connection, he changed the subject. "Mrs. Martin, when I called you on the phone, you asked me if I was going to arrest you." She nodded, wringing her hands. "What made you think you had done something so wrong that I would want to arrest you ... can you explain that?"

She looked at the floor, then, sheepishly, "I thought it was about the money."

Once, again, the two men exchanged glances. "What money?" asked the nephew.

Without answering, she arose, saying, "Excuse me, I'll be right back," and she disappeared into the hallway. The men stood and looked around the room. There were family pictures on the TV and on the mantel. There was one large one of Debra Barre', professionally done, and extremely striking. Mike looked at it for a long time. "God, but that woman was gorgeous. I can see how Marcel Gervais lost his head over her."

The older man grinned. "No, Michael, he lost his *life* over her." The woman had returned to the room and seeing the men looking at her dead sister, commented, "She was beautiful, wasn't she?" But then, pensively, "I think it was her beauty that cost her her life." She was carrying a duffel bag, the kind that people take to the health club. She placed it on the coffee table, and to both men, "That's the reason; the money in that bag."

Mike moved to the bag, and asked, "May I look inside?" to which she nodded. He slowly opened the bag, not quite sure what he would find. He looked inside, and whistled. "Oh, my God, Unck, look at this." The older man peeked in and saw the bag filled with hundred dollar bills, all neatly banded as they would come from a bank.

The younger man looked at the woman who was just sitting there, shaking her head, then asked, "Mrs. Martin, how much money is in here ... do you know?"

She nodded. "Yes, I counted it. There's over seventy thousand dollars there."

"Where did you get it? From Debra?" asked the uncle.

She smiled. "Where else would I get that kind of money? Oh, my God! What was that girl into?"

"But," the uncle persisted, "how did it come into your possession, I mean?"

The woman stood and walked to the fireplace, still twisting her hands, explaining, "Some time ago, Debra gave me a key to a safety deposit box to a bank in Golden Meadow. She told me that if anything ever happened to her, that I was to open the box and take whatever was in there, for it was now mine. I thought it might be some jewelry because she had some nice pieces, but this ... I just don't know. Where could she get that kind of money? My God! What was she involved in? Do you know?"

Mike shook his head. "No, Mrs. Martin, that is precisely what we are trying to find out."

The uncle added, "When we find that out, I believe we will know what this is all about, Mrs. Martin. Incidentally, was there anything else in that safety deposit box besides the money?"

Her eyes widened as if in horror. "Yes, that is what really scares me. There was an envelope in there, too," and extracting it from her pocket, she handed it to the nephew. He opened the flap which was not stuck any longer, having been opened by the sister, and withdrew two items, one a written note, and the other some kind of official-looking card, like a credit card in hard plastic. The note read:

"If anything ever happens to me, Nedra, honey, please know that I love you and Mama and want the best for you both. This cash will carry you over for a while, but there is more. Take this card with its coded number on it to a Mr. Haskell at the bank whose name appears on the bottom of the card. He will instruct you on what to do. It is all yours, honey, I love you. Debbie."

The nephew looked at the uncle, asking, "Is this what I think it is? I've never seen one. Have you?"

The older man nodded. "It is the code number to a Swiss Bank Account," and turning to the woman, he asked, "Mrs. Martin, did Debra ever mention a Swiss bank account to you?"

Nervously, "Oh, my God, no! What is this all about? I'm scared to death. I don't want any part of this."

"Mrs. Martin, did Debra have a will?"

She nodded. "Yes, she told me to talk to her lawyer in New Orleans, and he would tell me what to do. He has it, I believe. He called me the day after the shooting, saying he had to see me. I have an appointment with him on Wednesday. I'm scared to death."

Mike took her hand. "Mrs. Martin, since you will be in New Orleans, which is my jurisdiction, I will have to insist on going to the attorney's office with you."

She seemed relieved. "Oh, I would appreciate that! I really would. I don't know a thing about New Orleans."

Handing her his card, "You call me when you think you'll get to town and I will meet you at any place you choose. Will you be alone?"

"I guess so. My husband is out in the gulf and my four kids are in school, but thanks to Debbie, I have a good car so I guess I'll be OK if you will meet me at some place I can find. But, the money, what should I do with it? I don't want all that money in the house. I don't even know if I can keep it. Can I?"

It was the uncle who responded. "If your sister came about it honestly and the courts have no claim on it, then it is yours, but the courts will have to decide that, Mrs. Martin. I strongly suggest to you that you return the money to the safety deposit box until some legal disposition is made of it. If the money is legally yours, it will be awarded to you, I assure you."

Mike asked, "I understand that your sister visited you every other Wednesday, is that correct?"

She managed a weak smile. "Oh, yes, I enjoyed her visits so much. We'd go to Raceland to see Mama, who is not in good shape, you know, but she always perked up when she saw Debbie. She'd say, 'Oh, my baby, you're here.' She always said the same thing, and Debbie would cry, and then, we'd all have a cry. It was sad, but happy, if you know what I mean ..." and her voice trailed off.

Mike continued, "And she would spend the night with you—Wednesday night, that is?"

"Oh, yes, without fail. That is why she added her room to the house." She looked slightly embarrassed as she continued, "Debbie was used to more luxury than we had here, so she added her own bedroom. Would you like to see it? It's right here," and she pointed, once again, to the hallway. Both men nodded as she led the way. They entered a room which could only be described as opulent. It was not overly large, perhaps sixteen by twenty feet, with an entire wall of closets, all filled with clothes. The room had its own bath complete with a hot tub. The sister looked around proudly, picking up a photo of Debra on the dressing table, lovingly running her fingers over it, as she said, softly, "She was so beautiful," and then coming back to reality, "I told her she was spending too much money on one bedroom in a dinky old house, but she said, 'Nedra, honey, I've become accustomed to my own way of life. Why should I change it now?'"

The two men walked slowly around the room, making a mental note of all things they saw. Mike opened a few drawers and feeling he was intruding, he refrained from opening the others. He felt this room would tell them nothing except that she had access to a great deal of money, much more than her job as executive assistant to Jo-Jo Terrafina would justify. He headed out of the room, followed by his uncle and the sister, saying, "Mrs. Martin, I really don't think we should take any more of your time. You have been a great help—more than you know, I assure you. I thank you and I will await your phone call on the trip to New Orleans."

She seemed relieved for some reason. "Oh, I thank you for coming. I don't know why, but I feel better about this. Will you be able to find out who killed my sister?"

He took her hand, holding it warmly. "I surely hope so. But, you may not like the answers when I find them, I think I'd better warn you."

They had reached the family room by then, and she looked him straight in the eye. "Sergeant, I'm no fool. For a long time I've felt that Debbie was getting into something she had no business doing. Good girls don't make that kind of money, do they? She told me once that with her face and her body, she could get any man to do anything she wanted, and I told her, Debra, honey, if you believe that, you're heading for big trouble, and do you know what she told me? She said, 'That's where the big money is—where the big trouble is—they go together!'"

They reached the front door, with the uncle taking her hand, saying, "Mrs. Martin, it was a pleasure meeting you. I wish we could have met under more pleasant circumstances."

She blinked back tears. "I wish so, too, Mr. Guilbert," pronouncing it correctly, which pleased him greatly.

"One more thing, Madam, can you tell me where we can get some good fried catfish hereabouts?"

She seemed truly contrite. "Oh, I wish I had known you wanted some. I could've cooked you some. I still can if you want to wait. I have some already filleted, too."

He took her hand, again. "No, my dear lady, we can't allow you to do this, not with everything else on your mind. Perhaps, some other time, though."

"Just let me know. We don't stand on formality down here on the bayou, you know."

"Good-bye, and thank you for your hospitality."

As the car headed north along the bayou, Alcide Guilbert looked out the window, saying as much to himself as to his nephew, "Well, well, haven't we opened a hell of a can of worms?"

The nephew, deep in thoughts of his own, "We damn sure have, Unck that's for sure. Are you seeing any daylight, now?"

"Oh, yes ... plenty of daylight. We are having a good day, nephew. As a matter of fact, we are having a great day. I told you all along that this thing was not about sex alone, and believe me, it is not." He returned again to looking at the shrimp boats plying the narrow bayou, all escorted by the ubiquitous seagulls, screaming their cacophonous and dischorded melody.

He mused, philosophically, "You know, nephew, it is safe to say that two of the most powerful driving forces on this planet are," and he dragged the words out, "sex and money. And that is what this is all about, sex and money," and then bolting up, pointing in the direction of a small restaurant sitting partially over land and partially over water, exclaimed, "Look, there is our catfish place ... pull over!"

The nephew laughed, correcting him, "You left out good Cajun cooking as one of the real driving forces, too."

"How true, my boy, how true!"

CHAPTER SEVEN

TUESDAY MORNING

The lear jet circled low over the marsh south of Harry P. Williams Memorial airport near Patterson, LA, as it approached it from the west. The jet had crossed the US-Mexico border at McAllen, Texas, and through the experience of the pilot, who was experienced at drug smuggling from countries to the south, had managed a very weak customs inspection at that port of entry. After refueling, the sleek craft headed east toward the coast of south Louisiana, carrying a weary and disgruntled passenger. He was as highly upset as he ever allowed his well disciplined mind to indulge in, as he looked forward to his new assignment without relish. When he had landed in Madrid on last Friday night, after a nonstop flight from Boston, he looked forward to a month of relaxation on the French Riviera, as he had promised himself, but when he went to the office of his "booking agent" to receive the last half of his fee, the bad news was waiting.

In fluent Spanish, he asked, incredulously, "Go back for another job? Are you crazy? That is one way to get killed. I never go back to the same place! Get someone else to do it."

The agent put a fatherly arm around his shoulder. "Now, that is not possible, my friend. They want you, and no one but you. They liked the way you did the job—real clean, the way they like it."

"No! I will not go back. I refuse!"

"Now, amigo, you know you cannot refuse these people. You are in too deep. They can take care of you just as you took care of those unfortunate people. Besides, they knew you would balk, so they have doubled the price, and they promise they will not bother you for at least a month, maybe two."

He walked over to the window, looking out on a beautiful plaza where amorous Latin couples nuzzled each other in the Iberian sun while children played nearby. He turned back to the agent. "But, do you know how long it will take to get airline reservations and all that?"

"Yes, we have taken care of all that. They have agreed to fly you over on a company jet, direct from here to Cape Verde, then to Caracas, and then to Belize City. From there, a Lear jet to northern Mexico and across the border into the U.S. The pilot on the Lear will have instructions as to where to go from there."

"Who is my target?" he asked, coldly.

"It's all here in the packet, complete with photos, schedules, just as before. It is very complete."

"And how will I get back? Will the jet wait for me?"

"No, that is too risky. You will go to the waterfront the same day, as explained in the packet. A Spanish ship of Liberian registry will be sailing that same afternoon. The captain of the ship is expecting you. You will sail that evening, and he will discharge you in the Caymans, where you are free to take any means you wish to get back here."

He returned to take the packet from his agent's hand, asking, "And you say they will double the price?"

"Yes. Fifty thousand dollars for an afternoon's work, plus five thousand expense money as before, all in used hundred dollar bills."

He could feel the adrenaline flowing as he replied, "I'll do it, but this is the last one for two months."

As the Lear lined up on runway five, he could see through the pilot's windshield that this was a relatively small field, without a control tower. No wonder they picked it, he thought. Landing at a New Orleans airport would have been more convenient, but they all had control towers. The Lear used only a portion of the 5300-foot concrete runway, turning back to the FBO at the small field used mostly by the oil industry, and parked in front of the small terminal. He alighted with his two bags, one B-4 bag and his oversize briefcase. He rented a small car, and offered a gold credit card on a fictious but solvent nonperson the company kept current for him. He received instructions on the shortest route to New Orleans and he headed out on Highway 90 East.

He had not had time to change his appearance as much as he would have liked, but he had had time to dye his hair a light blond. He also had time to install a set of blue contact lenses to hide his natural brown eyes. Now he looked like any American ski bum one would meet on the ski slopes of Vail or Aspen. He looked at his watch. It was 9:00am, Tuesday morning, less than a week since he had been in Louisiana for his last contract. He had read of his work in papers all along the route. He was proud of himself. He had done a good job, and now, for being so efficient, he was asked to do the same thing again, in the same town. He had not even had time to study his packet. He didn't need much time, really. They told him to be at a particular place at a particular time, and to kill the person identified in the photo. It was as simple as that. They never went into details for they knew that was up to him. That was his job.

He crossed the Mississippi at Luling and after a few miles on the Airline Highway, he pulled into the car return area of New Orleans International airport and turned in the rental car. He then went immediately to a different car rental agency and, using a different card and a different name, he rented another car. He exited the airport, crossed the Airline and went into the Airport Hilton across the street from the airport. He went to the restroom, refreshed himself, and walked into the dining room for his midday meal. As he sipped on a glass of Chablis, he removed the packet from his jacket pocket. He withdrew the material and began to peruse it. His eyebrows went up as he saw the target. He shook his head in disbelief. He shuffled the papers to make sure this was no mistake, but it was not. The instructions were quite complete. The target always left his office around the same time, four o'clock, and he was driven to his club, where he mixed with some cronies until around six o'clock and then, he went out to eat at the same restaurant each weekday night. He mused, "habits can kill you."

He watched the other diners as they went about their business of eating, drinking and socializing. He resented their apparent contentment, for having never experienced the feeling, himself, he had no reference to go by. He was not even sure he knew what happiness was. He was not even sure he wanted to know. He was content with being miserable.

He wiped his mouth, extracted his wallet, and left a three dollar tip on the table, exactly fifteen percent of his tab. As he sat in his car, he looked at his watch. Plenty time! He took out his map of New Orleans. He had studied it in detail on his last trip, as he always did in case he needed to make a fast getaway. He saw how St. Claude Ave. ran into Esplanade and he knew where Esplanade was. He took the airport short cut to I-10 and headed east into the city. He exited the Interstate on Claiborne and he could see the Central Police Lockup. He smiled, as he thought, "If only they knew who was back in town, and for what purpose ..."

He found Esplanade with no trouble and turned on St. Claude, heading southeasterly for quite some time, checking the house numbers as he drove slowly down the street. When he saw that he was approaching the block of numbers given him, he found a place to park. He locked his bags in the car and began to survey the neighborhood. He knew that he would only get one shot so he could not afford an error. He also knew that if he got a good shot, that would be all he would need. He could see the address of his target, but he needed a vantage point from which he would not be seen, and one from which he could make a quick retreat without being seen by any witnesses, and one that would give him quick access to the city. He saw an old apartment building about one hundred yards from the expected target location. That was a little farther than he would have liked, but it would have to do. It had a set of steel steps leading to a typical New Orleans balcony with cheap, imitation French Quarter grillwork. He climbed the stairs and looked in the direction of the target. The line of sight was not all that good, but he saw none better. As he stood there for a moment, a door opened to one of the apartments. A young woman came out in shorts and T-shirt, giving him a seductive look, saying, "Hi. Nice day, isn't it?"

He had not planned on this interference, but he had no choice but to be civil or risk suspicion from her. He smiled. "Yes, nice day," avoiding the "r's". She walked over to him, giving him a once over, then, feeling that she had gauged him correctly, she asked, "Are you looking for a little fun, honey?"

He had definitely not counted on that. Even if he had been without female company for several weeks, she would never have qualified if he had been in the mood. He found her somewhat repulsive, but he needed this vantage point. He looked at his watch. It was only 2:30pm. He had an hour and a half to kill before his target would appear. Without relish, he managed a half smile. "What did you have in mind?"

She came even closer, confident that she had a likely quarry on what had been a very slow day. She smiled, touching his arm. "Well, I thought we'd get out of this heat and go in my place and have a cool beer, or something," she said with as much promise as she could muster. He glanced at his watch again, asking, "How much will this cost, or is it free?"

She giggled, "Free? Honey, are you serious? I do this for a living. I'll admit you're cute, but cute don't get it when the rent is due, know what I mean?"

"I know what you mean. How much?"

She tried to size him up for her prices were negotiable, depending on circumstances. She replied, coyly, "Well, it depends on what you want and how long you want it."

"I don't have much time ... just time for a quickie."

Disappointed, she replied, "Oh. Well, I can let you have a straight quickie for fifty dollars."

"How about twenty-five?"

"Forty."

"Thirty."

Sensing she was losing his interest, if she ever had it, she reluctantly replied, "OK, thirty, but don't expect anything sensational, if you know what I mean."

He tried to see how this unexpected turn of events would fit into his plans. His experienced mind went over all eventualities. He knew he had to play for time, so he said, "Look, I have some bags I need to get. They're in my friend's car and he is coming to get the car, so I have to get my bags out. Can I bring them in your apartment?"

She thought for a while. "Sure, but that will cost five dollars ... for storage, you know ... "

He smiled at her pettiness. "Agreed. I'll get my bags," and he bounded down the steps towards the rental car, which he never intended to return anyway. He took the B-4 bag and the briefcase out, locked the car, and pocketed the keys, just in case his plans were changed. When he reached the apartment door, she was waiting and smiling, kidding, "It looks like you're traveling. Say, you're not on the run, are you? I don't want anything to do with you if the cops are after you."

"No, I have a flight out tonight, that's all."

"Oh, well, I guess that's OK, then. I'll just slip into something more comfortable. Why don't you get us a couple of beers out of the fridge. It's all in the price, you know," and she disappeared into the bathroom. He shrugged and grinned. What the hell, he thought, might as well make the most of it.

As she came out, now devoid of all pretense of salesmanship, she quipped, "Well, let's get with it, honey. If this is going to be a quickie, you know you get what you pay for," and with that she threw herself on the bed, beckoning him with both arms. As she had promised, it was uninspiring to say the least. She attempted to put on an act, but she was also a bad actress. He suffered through the ordeal on pure animalistic fervor, and as the fluids of life flowed out of him, he placed both hands on her throat and without emotion or any sign of remorse, squeezed the life out of her. She gurgled her last as he raised himself from the motionless corpse. He stood there for a moment, looking at her with distaste, cursing the luck that placed him in this situation, then, looking at his watch to ensure that he had time, he proceeded to the bathroom and took a shower. He dressed, and walking to the window, he realized that this could have been a stroke of luck after all. The apartment window offered him an excellent view of the target area without his being seen by any passerby. It had the added advantage of being on the side of the building away from the balcony. Now, no one could see the barrel of the rifle protruding as he took aim. He would wait here until the appointed time, and then, do the job and leave by the back stair. Yes, he mused, it should work out fine. He glanced back at the nude body of the girl lying in the bed, her

Lloyd J. Guillory

face contorted by the struggle to breathe. He went to the bed and coldly drew the sheet over the body. He heard a knock on the door. A female voice called, "Lurline, it's Shirley. Are you home?"

His breathing became more pronounced. He didn't need this at all. He waited. She called out once more, and feeling her friend was not home, she left, much to his satisfaction. He completed dressing, then, he placed the briefcase on the table. He removed the sections of the .257 Roberts Mauser rifle. He screwed the barrel into the threaded recess, a product of milling by a master craftsman. He extracted three cartridges from the case and he looked at them. They were of the 100 gram expanding type, with a muzzle velocity of 2900 feet per second and a muzzle energy of 1870 foot pounds of energy. He placed all three in the stock magazine and pulled the bolt back, forcing one into the chamber. He walked to the window and slid back the sliding panel which had a screen on the exterior. He took out a knife and cut the fiberglass screen very easily. He had an unobstructed view of the target area. He raised the rifle and looked through the 4 power scope and convinced himself that he had as good a vantage point as possible. He turned to the dead girl and mentally thanked her for making this possible. He lowered the rifle, running his hands lovingly over its vanadium steel barrel. He leaned it against the wall. He could feel the adrenaline flowing as the appointed time drew near. He looked at his watch. It was nearly four o'clock. He raised the rifle, again, and waited. He could feel the pounding of his heart in his chest.

He now saw a long black limousine pull up to the curb and two men jumped out, looking in all directions. One man nodded to another and he went in the building. The driver and the other man were leaning against the limo, joking and talking. Several minutes passed with nothing happening. He was getting nervous. He didn't like anything to go off schedule; it made him nervous. Then, the door to the building opened and two men came out, laughing and joking. He had no difficulty in identifying the subject, for he was not wearing a hat and the others were. The two wearing hats looked in all directions, and suspecting nothing, nodded to the man without the hat. He stood there for a moment, talking to one of the men. The rifle was raised until the cross hairs in the scope fell directly between the subject's eyes. Then, the trigger was squeezed and in the fraction of a second that it took the bullet to travel the 300 feet, the top of Jo-Jo Terrafina's head blew off and flew into space, splattering the two bodyguards near him. They fell to the ground, just as he did, but for different reasons: he was dead, and they were frightened. Lying on the ground, afraid to rise, they drew their revolvers in defense. One looked and pointed in one direction, and the other pointed in the opposite direction. People in the warehouse of Coastal Produce came running out, knowing very well what the sound meant. Panic began to form as each person swore, still crouching in fear, that they had heard the shot come from ten different places. The assassin coolly and quickly unscrewed the barrel and scope, replaced the weapons in the case, picked up his bags, then put them down again, wiped off finger prints from everything he had touched including the girl's throat, and then exited by the back fire escape, out of sight of the dead and scared. He walked through side streets and alleys until he was on Rampart.

As luck would have it, he saw a Metro cab coming in his direction. Seeing a man standing in the middle of the street with two bags by his side led the cabby to believe he had a large fare to New Orleans International. When the driver found out he didn't, he complained, "I'm on my way to another fare. You'll have to get another cab." But a twenty-dollar bill changed his mind. He entered the cab, throwing his bags in the back seat and climbing in the same seat, telling the cabby, "The French Quarter, the corner of St. Peter and St. Ann." As he put his head back on the seat, he finally began to breathe normally, but he could still feel his heart beating at a fast rate. The cabby said, "Nice day, ain't it?"

He smiled. "Yes, a good day," avoiding the "r's".

As they drove off, the sounds of sirens could be heard coming from the direction of St. Claude. The cabby remarked, "Something big must have happened on St. Claude," to which he replied, "Uh-huh."

At the corner of Jackson Square, he exited the cab, taking the two bags with him. He paid the fare plus a five dollar tip. He felt generous. He had just made fifty thousand dollars. He lugged the bags into the Cafe DuMonde, placing them under a table. He ordered coffee and beignets and relaxed as he ate without conscience or remorse. Finished, he picked up his bags and walked out of the cafe. He walked out to the Moonwalk, climbed the stairs to the river walk, and proceeded down river to a large vessel he saw tied up at the Nicholls Street wharf. He looked up at the name on the stern: LOS PALOMAS ... MADRID. He smiled as he walked to the gangplank. He looked up and saw a man in a nautical uniform looking down at him, a man with four stripes on his epaulets. The captain smiled down at him, saying "Buenos tarde, Senor. Es usted, Senor Esteban?"

"Si," he replied, "Es mio."

The captain waved him up with, "Mi casa es su casa. Bien venido." He recognized the pre-agreed greeting as stipulated in his instructions and he breathed easier.

At that moment the steam whistle on the ship gave a deep throated

Lloyd J. Guillory

groan, and as the captain waved a signal to a man in the bridge, the port tugs began to move the huge craft away from the wharf, edging it out into the mighty river, where the river pilots would take it out to the mouth of the river. There, they would return control of the craft to its captain and it would start its journey to the Cayman Islands.

He made his way to a cabin reserved for him in the officer's section. He threw himself on the bed, telling the steward in his fluent Spanish, "Wake me for supper," and he immediately fell asleep.

CHAPTER EIGHT

WEDNESDAY MORNING

Once, again, the journalistically reticent *Times-Picayune* morning paper had glaring headlines concerning the murder of Jo-Jo Terrafina the day before, and as in the case of the previous murder of Marcel Gervais and Debra Barre', a subheadline told of the murder of the alleged prostitute, Sandra (Sunny) Dey. It read in only smaller print: Woman Murdered in Same Block, and then it asked: Connection???

The police lost no time, however, in confirming that there was, indeed, a connection between the two murders, when it was ascertained that the fatal shot could have been fired from one angle only and that was in the apartment of the dead woman. But, they asked themselves, "Was he in the apartment to purposely kill the woman, or, was she just in the wrong place at the wrong time?"

Captain Monahan nervously bit on a pencil because his lip was already sore from the excessive biting it endured while he was in the office of the commissioner late the night before. The commissioner had bloodshot eyes from his visit to the mayor's office, when the mayor had passed on the heat he had gotten, indirectly, the night before on the ten o'clock news. The town was in an uproar and even the man in the street who generally accepted a murder a day as the norm began to say in their best Irish Channel accent, "Geez, what da hell is goin on in dis town?" In the coffee shops of some of the best hotels in town, as well as the bars in the French Quarter, the citizenry were perplexed. Prior to the Terrafina murder, most had felt they had it all figured out, and it was only a matter of time before the police would confirm their conclusions: "It's an open and shut case. The blueblood got caught wit his hand in the cookie jar, so to speak, and the boyfriend took revenge. Who could blame him? I'da done the same thing if my broad had done dat to me." But, now, with the demise of Jo-Jo, the citizenry were confused, "What the hell is going on in this town?" and that is precisely what the mayor had asked the commissioner, the commissioner had asked the captain, and, now, the captain was asking the man in charge of the case, Mike Fortier: "Fortier, what the hell is going on in this town?"

He, too, nervously bit his lip as he raised his hands. "Gee, I thought I had this thing about figured out before Jo-Jo got his brains blown out, but now I don't know!"

The captain got out of his chair, walked to the window, looked out at the traffic in the street, and turned to the sergeant who looked depressed, asking, "Mike, what have you got so far? Fill me in, so I can pass it on to the top."

"Well, I thought at least the evidence was beginning to point to some kind of trouble that Gervais had gotten himself into ... business trouble."

The captain, trying to remain calm while he was not, interrupted, "So Marcel Gervais was in some kind of trouble? How the hell does the Barre' girl fit in this thing? Tell me that!"

"I'm not sure, yet, but I think she helped him get in trouble, or, she got him in it ... "

Another interruption. "Hell, Mike, when a broad entices a married man as prominent as Marcel Gervais to join her in a role in the hay, he is already in trouble with some people, especially his wife."

He shook his head in protest. "No, Captain, I don't mean that kind of trouble. I mean real trouble, big trouble!"

The captain, perplexed, "What the hell kind of trouble are you talking about that could get them killed?"

He sighed, "I don't know, yet. I need more time to put the pieces together, " and he filled the captain in on the conversations with the dead girl's sister, the money, the Swiss bank account—all of it. His response was, "Jesus! What the hell have we got here?" and looking his sergeant in the eye, "Maybe, Mike, this thing is getting too big for us," and scratching his chin as he always did when he was perplexed, he added, "Maybe we ought to call in the FBI for help."

Mike, seeing the case slip away from him, asked with some apprehension, "But, how can we justify that? We don't know if any federal laws have been broken?" Give me some more time on this, Captain ... I'll crack it, I swear!"

The captain shook his head as he walked around the room. "I don't know, Mike, this thing is getting bigger all the time. I think you need some help on it," and as he walked back to the window, again, adding, "we need someone like your uncle, Alcide, on this thing. Damn, I wish he hadn't retired," and walking directly to the sergeant, asked, "Do you think he would come back to work on this thing? He loved this kind of case, the tougher the better." Walking back to his desk, he sat down, and looked at the sergeant. "I'll make a deal with you, Mike. If you can get your uncle to help you on this case, I'll leave it in your hands for another week, but that is all the time you got, no more? If you can't crack it by then, I'll call in the FBI and tell them we have reason to believe a federal crime was committed."

He looked up, exasperated. "What federal crime?"

"Hell, I don't know! I'll make up one. Now, what do you think about getting your uncle in on the case. Will he do it?"

Mike smiled, inwardly. "Well, I don't know. He's retired and enjoying life. I just don't know ... "

"Well, would it hurt to ask him? I heard from a mutual friend of ours that all he does all day is sit home and watch TV and complain about his arthritis and hemorrhoids."

Mike could not suppress a smile at this as he replied, "Well, he's earned a right to do that."

"Fortier, why do I get the impression that you are reluctant to ask your uncle for help in this case?"

He shrugged. "Because of your promise to me."

"What promise?"

"You promised if I cracked this case, you'd see that I would get a promotion to lieutenant."

The captain nodded, grinning, "So, that's the problem, huh? You feel with your uncle on the case, you'd end up not getting all the glory or your promotion?"

He fidgeted. "Well, yeah, that's true. I told my wife about the promotion, and she got all excited, and, well ... "

The captain, anxious to bring the meeting to an end, pointed his pencil at him, replying, "Look, Mike, if you can talk Alcide into helping you, and you crack this thing within a week, I'll keep my promise to you, I swear," and in an after thought, "You don't think Alcide would try to steal your thunder, would you? You know what I mean ... with the press and all, do you?"

Mike grinned. "I guess that's my problem, Captain. I'll talk to him and see what he says. If he agrees, is he officially on the case? He'll ask about money, you know."

The captain smiled. "Tell the old bastard he will be drawing consultant's pay—no deductions, and the usual out-of-pocket expenses. Now, get the hell out of here and go to work. You got a week—that's all, and then the Feds come in."

He could hardly wait to get to the uncle's house to tell him of the captain's offer, smiling all the way. As he related the meeting to his uncle, the old man grinned as he puffed on his pipe, asking, "And what did he say to that? And what did you say? No shit? Consultant's pay ... and an expense account?"

"That's right, Unck. You're back on the force. What do you say?"

He grinned. "Why not! With Rosalie coming back to town, I can use the extra money. That way, I won't have to cash any more CDs. Yeah, I'll do it—for you and Cindy and the kids," he said, looking for some excuse he could accept himself.

The nephew asked, "What do you think of the Terrafina killing? Any ideas?"

He nodded, lighting his pipe, and then puffing hard, "Yeah, I have some ideas, but nothing you can hang your hat on. I'll bet you one thing, though, those killings are all related, except for that poor little hooker. She just happened to proposition the wrong man at the wrong time, that's all. Once again, Mike, her killing wasn't about sex. It was something else."

"Do you think the same man did it?"

"I don't know. Any witnesses on this one?"

"Yeah, a pretty good one, too. A cab driver picked up a man shortly after the killing, just a block from the girl's apartment. He jumped in the cab with two bags—the cabby noticed that—one military-style B-4 bag and a large briefcase."

"Any good description?"

"Yeah, he said the man was about six feet, blond, with blue eyes."

"That confuses that issue, doesn't it?" the uncle rejoined.

"What do you mean?"

He puffed on the pipe, and finding it out, he arose and went through the elaborate lighting ritual as he furrowed his brow, "You know, I've narrowed the guest list from the Royal Orleans down to two people: the foreign looking character, Emile Rashid, and the other ... Nick Bono. They were both brunettes. Did you look into Rashid's not checking out like I asked you to?"

He nodded. "Well, I put a man on it. He said the desk clerk remembers Emile Rashid real well. Said he was the kind of man you can't forget, sort of a character. He paid in advance for the room with two one hundred dollar bills which he took out of a little leather pouch, you know, how those little ladies used to do years ago. Well, he stayed there two nights and the bill would have come to just about that amount with tax, so when he didn't check out, the hotel just assumed he was satisfied with the money situation, and they were, too. Actually, he had some change coming back, so they threw it in petty cash."

The old man replied, "Uh huh, and what of the other fellow, Nick Bono?"

"Well, the records show that he paid with two one hundred dollar traveler's checks, and he checked out."

"Do you have any idea where they went, then? Either of them?"

"We know that Nick Bono boarded a plane for Memphis, but we lost him there. The Memphis address he gave was a fake. The airports, the rentals, the bus station—nothing. He just disappeared as if he never existed."

The uncle, now that his pipe was functioning, puffed hard, blowing a series of smoke rings towards the ceiling, replying with some relish, "That's because he never existed."

"What do you mean, never existed?"

"Because, my boy, I'll bet you ten bucks when we solve this thing, if we ever do, you will find that Emile Rashid and Nick Bono are one and the same people."

"How the hell do you know that?"

"I don't know for sure. I just surmise ... that's all, and now that we have hashed this out, what do you intend to do today to earn your pay?"

"Have you forgotten that I promised to go to the attorney's office with Mrs. Martin?"

He nodded. "Ah, yes, that should be an interesting meeting, from which we should learn plenty about Debra Barre', and perhaps, even something about Marcel Gervais. Who knows?"

"What are *you* going to do to earn your pay, Unck, now that you are on the payroll again?"

He knocked the burned tobacco out of his pipe. "I am going to lunch today at the Petroleum Club."

"The hell you say! You call that working? And, how can you lunch at the Petroleum Club? Don't you have to be a member to go there?"

"Yes, to all your questions! Yes, I'll be working, and yes, you have to be a member, unless you are the guest of a member, which I will be. I called an old geologist friend from my college days. He is a member, and I suggested to him that it would be a good idea if he invited me to lunch at the Club, and he graciously consented."

Curious, the nephew asked, "And what do you propose to learn there?"

"I propose to learn a lot about the oil business, especially about Tradewind Drilling. I feel that Marcel Gervais's venture into the oil business might be pertinent to this case, quite pertinent and relevant to be precise. And now, enough of this idle chatter. You go your way and I will go mine. Pick me up at five this evening, here, and we'll compare notes."

Alcide Guilbert could be a charming man when he chose to, and he

Lloyd J. Guillory

was charming at lunch with his old friend Carter Blatner, with whom he had played a great deal of golf in earlier days he referred to as "prearthritic".

As the lunch wore on and they skirted the reason for his being there, Blatner asked, "Alcide, my old friend, as pleasant as it is to see you, again, I know you well enough to know that this is not simply a rejuvenation of an old friendship. You haven't called me in several years," and he smiled, warmly, "so, what is it you want of me at this time?"

He grinned. "Carter, you always were the suspicious type. Do I have to have ulterior motives simply because I asked you to invite me to lunch?" he smiled.

"Yes, Alcide, you do. You'll always be a detective at heart, so what is it you are trying to detect, today?"

He smiled. "I plead guilty, Carter," and as he poured himself more coffee, and offering to do the same for his host, he continued. "It concerns the Gervais case," and with his newly acquired authority of that day, he continued, "I am helping the department in this matter." He stirred his coffee. "We have been informed that Marcel Gervais, in the past year or so, jumped into the oil drilling business, and we understand the deal might have turned sour, so," and he sipped the coffee, "we want to look into it. Can you help me on that one?"

The geologist sighed. "You know, I wish people who know nothing of the oil game would stay the hell out of it. They just muddy the water and make it tough for those of us who make a living at it."

He shrugged. "I'm sure that could be said for anyone who gets out of his niche, his element, so to speak. Do you have any details on Tradewind Drilling?"

He shook his head. "No, not details, but it was well known around the oil patch that Marcel had made a big mistake in getting into it. What I could never understand was, why would a man with his family wealth want to get into a drilling venture with the likes of Grover Canton."

"So, you know of Mr. Canton?"

He looked around the room. "Who in the oil business has not heard of that shyster? He has a reputation for selling leases two or more times, if he can swing it."

"Yes, I know of him. What do you know of Tradewind Drilling?"

"Look, Alcide, I don't know any details that would be considered credible, but there is a man over there who should know a lot about it," and he nodded in a direction of the wall. "His name is Albert Walters, a retired doctor. He is one of the limited partners in the deal, and a very unhappy one, too."

"Would you introduce me to him?"

"No, not if you're going to interrogate him in the Gervais matter. He might resent the introduction and it would affect our friendship. Is there any reason you can't approach him directly? After all, you're a policeman, Alcide, and a well-known one at that."

He sighed. "Well, I guess that is the way it will have to be done, my friend. I want to thank you for the invitation, Carter. I apologize for the imposition. How about lunch on me, Wednesday, next week...at Commander's Palace?"

"Without ulterior motives?"

He smiled. "None whatsoever! Just friendship."

"Commander's Palace, huh? That's a pricey place, you know."

Thinking of his new found expense account, he replied, "Uh-huh, I know, but that is the value I place on your friendship, Carter."

"Oh, bullshit, Alcide, but I'll show up."

With a good-bye to his host, the old detective made his way to the table of Dr. Albert Walters, who was just winding up his lunch with a group of friends. He walked over to the man who had been pointed out to him by his geologist friend as one of the limited partners in the drilling venture. He stood next to the retired doctor who, looking up, asked, "May I help you?"

Alcide smiled awkwardly, hating to resort to bad manners, but felt justified under the circumstance, "Please excuse me, Doctor Walters, my name is Alcide Guilbert, and I am with the NOPD. I wonder if I may have a word or two with you when you have finished your lunch. I am perfectly willing to wait until you have finished."

The doctor smiled. "Your fame has preceded you, Inspector Guilbert. Then, smiling for the benefit of his table companions, "Am I in trouble with the law?"

He returned the smile. "No, I can assure you that you are not, doctor. I want to ask you about Tradewind Drilling, that's all."

The doctor could not suppress a loud laugh. "Oh, if that is what you want, Inspector, you have picked a most propitious time," and he waved a hand at the other three men at the table. "You are looking at four members of that unfortunate venture. As a matter of fact, that is what this luncheon is all about. We are commiserating about Marcel's death and where it leaves us. Please, grab a chair and join us, and we will tell you all about Tradewind Drilling," and turning to the other men, "Won't we, gentlemen?"

"It was not my intent to intrude upon your meeting. I told you, doctor, that I would be willing to wait until you are finished."

"Oh, come on, sit down. You are not intruding. We need to talk to someone about this. We don't know where we're going with this thing now that our leader and partner, Marcel, is gone. Incidentally, have you solved the case yet? Do you know who killed our partner? And the latest killing—who did that? My God, this place is like Beirut," and the other men nodded and laughed.

Alcide laughed, in accommodation, although he did not think it too funny since it reflected on the police department, of which he was now a newly reinstated member. "It would seem that way, as of late," and clearing his throat, he said, "I was hoping that you gentlemen could tell me a little about Tradewind Drilling ... if you are willing."

It was one of the others who replied, "Well, you could subpoena us and have us deposed, could you not?"

He nodded. "Yes, I suppose so, but I would prefer to keep it friendly," and he added, "for the time being anyway."

The doctor, being by far the most loquacious of the group, looked at the others, then began, "Well, it all started out as a joke, I suppose. On the golf course, one day we all," and he waved all around, "used to golf together. Well, someone mentioned how good the seafood was here at the Petroleum Club, and someone else said, 'Sure, that is fine if you are a member,' and then someone else said, 'What we need is an oil well, and then we could become members,' ... just a joke, you know. We thought nothing more of it until one day Marcel called us all and asked to meet him for lunch. I might add, inspector, that all of us are professional men, and we are of some," and he cleared his throat, "substance" if you know what I mean. We're not exactly on food stamps."

Alcide Guilbert smiled. "I understand. Please continue."

"Well, when we got there, there was Marcel with this character, Grover Canton. None of us knew him, or of him. Believe me, I wish to hell we had. We depended on Marcel." He stopped and called a waiter. "Rubin, would you bring us some fresh coffee, please? Thank you. Anyway, I will try to shorten this story, because it could be long and drawn out. This guy, Grover Canton tells us he has gotten his hands on some real hot oil leases in the prairie country near Mamou." He laughed. "I know you've heard the song, 'Big Mamou', and the others smirked. "Well, we were as green as grass about the oil drilling industry, but when this smooth talking bastard, Canton, got finished telling us about depletion allowances, production for the next fifty years, and all that crap, and all we had to do was put up five thousand dollars a piece ... well, we got interested. We formed, on his advice, a limited partnership with Marcel as the general partner. We would have nothing to do but sit back and wait for the well to blow."

There was general laughter all around the table, in addition to

Summary Justice

smirks, as he continued, "Well, it seemed that the five thousand dollars were only to purchase the leases from Canton, and did not include drilling, which was to cost another ten thousand a piece. It seemed he had a friend who had a friend who had a cheap drilling rig ... that kind of crap. We were permitted to drill down to eight thousand five hundred feet to a supposedly good sand stratum. At least, that is what that half-ass, self proclaimed geologist, Canton, told us." The coffee had arrived and each man poured himself a cup, offering some to the inspector. The doctor sipped his, then, "Well, and now I get to the sad part, and the part that proves what dumb bastards we all are," and the others nodded. "That sand at eight thousand five hundred feet, proved to be of 'not producible quality' as it was called, but there were several other good sands at thirteen and fifteen thousand feet that we could not go wrong on ... if we would only come up with more money ... "

"How much more money?" asked the inspector.

They all grumbled, as the doctor answered, "Ten thousand each, and it got worse. Canton told us we would have to get more partners to cover the added cost of going that deep because we were talking big money to drill deep. Now, up till now, we each had fifteen thousand dollars in the deal. It would not have broken us to walk away, but what the hell, pride came into it. All of us big mouths had boasted to our wives and kids and family that we were about to hit an oil well, and we didn't want to look like bigger fools than we had been, so we enlarged the partnership to include ten partners, with each of us bringing in our brothers, brothers-in-law ... that sort of thing."

Alcide Guilbert shook his head. "Didn't any of you see the handwriting on the wall, that this might be a scam?

They nodded, some of them, but one answered, "Hell, we depended on Marcel Gervais. Here was a real smart guy, with impeccable credentials and he kept telling us it would turn out all right. Well, it didn't! When we got down to thirteen thousand feet, we had the well perforated and the geologist told us it was not a 'commercially producible sand', in their jargon. Well, we were some upset, especially, when this guy Canton told us we would have to come up with at least twenty thousand dollars, apiece to bring this well in. He swore on his dead mother's grave that the consulting geologists we had hired had confirmed that at eighteen thousand feet, there was a sand thirty feet thick, loaded with oil."

Alcide was incredulous. "You believed him?"

They shook their heads in unison. "No," the doctor answered, "we had had enough ... with the shyster, Canton, and quite frankly, with our friend Marcel Gervais, too. We had counted on him, and he had let us down. We were furious with him and told him so. As a matter of fact, we had informed him that we were seriously considering legal action against both of them. He nearly panicked at that. He said, if we sued him at this time, it would ruin him because of the large project he was heavily involved in. Had to do with some of this gambling casino crap that this state is involved in, as you are well aware. He said the bad publicity would kill the project because he was the general partner in that and the state would never grant a license to the casino if he had his picture spread all over the papers and TV on a bad deal. He was panicky. I've known Marcel for years, but I've never seen him as nervous as that. He begged us not to sue him. He promised that he would put up the money to complete the well, and that if it were successful, we would be repaid off the top.

"Did you folks agree to that?"

He looked around the table, as if embarrassed. "Well, sure, what the hell did we have to lose, other than what we had already put in the deal."

"So, what happened after that?" asked the inspector.

They looked at each other with dismay. "What happened?" asked the doctor. "The crazy bastard gets himself killed playing around with a woman who is some racketeer's girlfriend, and you ask what happened!" he responded too loud, for others at adjoining tables were looking.

"No, that is not what I meant," replied the inspector, calmly, "what is the status of the venture?"

They looked at each other, again, with each shrugging his shoulders, and the doctor replying, "That's what we want to know ... where do we stand? We're waiting for the dust to settle, and then we'll go at his estate, I can assure you."

Alcide asked, "Did Marcel Gervais ever come up with that big money? The one he said he would cover, himself?"

They nodded. "As far as I know, he did, because they were drilling at the time of his death, we know that."

"How much money are we talking about?"

"You mean all together, or just the amount he put in at the end?"

"No, just the big money at the end?"

The doctor shrugged. "I don't know for sure, but I would guess it had to run over two hundred thousand, at least."

The inspector drove his spike home. "Could he have covered that out of his own personal finances?"

One of the men who had been silent during the whole conversation spoke up, "No, not without liquidating some of his assets, or his wife's help, he couldn't. He had put out a lot of money to get a foothold on the casino project, and he was strapped. The firm had money, but Irving Stern would never have let him use that, not Irving."

Summary Justice

Alcide looked at the man, asking, "You seem to be speaking with some first-hand knowledge of his finances. May I inquire, sir, as to ... "

The man nodded. "I'm his stockbroker, but I will not—can not—answer any more questions about Mr. Gervais's finances until I speak to his lawyers and mine."

Alcide nodded. "I understand, and I agree with you," and turning to the entire group, he said as he rose, "Gentlemen, you have been a great help to me, I assure you, and I am grateful to you all. I hope in a week or so we can all have the answers to this complex situation, but until then, all we can do is continue to dig," and he smiled, "just as you continued to drill for oil, hoping you would strike pay dirt," and turning to leave, "Good day, gentlemen."

CHAPTER NINE

Mike had received a phone call from Nedra Martin the night before, just as he and Cindy were preparing for bed. It was Cindy who had answered the phone and upon hearing the female voice asking for "Sergeant Mike Fortier, please", she could not suppress a smile, "It's for you, Sergeant Fortier ... a woman," she teased. He patted her on her buns as he took the receiver from her, with, "Who is it?" he asked. Cindy shrugged, raising her eyebrows, and then walked off smiling at him, coquetishly. He grinned. "Sergeant Fortier, here, may I help you?"

"Yes, this is Nedra Martin ... remember, you told me to call about tomorrow?"

"Yes, of course, Mrs. Martin. I've been waiting for your call," and he winked at his wife who had her head sticking out of their bedroom door. She went into the room as Mike continued. "Are you still coming to the city tomorrow?"

"Yes, that is why I'm calling. Where do you want me to meet you? I don't know New Orleans very well at all. I took Mama to Hotel Dieu a couple of times when she needed surgery, but that is all."

"Yes, I know. Why don't you come in on the Luling bridge, and meet me in the lobby of the Airport Hilton. You can't miss it—it's directly across the highway from the airport. You know where the airport is, don't you?"

"Oh, yes, I can find that. What time?"

"What time is your appointment with the attorney?"

"At ten o'clock."

"That's fine. Can you meet me in the lobby no later than nine thirty?"

She laughed. "That's no problem. I'm a country girl. I get up and make coffee at five every morning."

"Good. I'll see you at nine thirty. Goodnight, Mrs. Martin."

As he entered their bedroom Cindy was standing there, smiling. She walked to their bed, pulled back the sheets, and beckoned to him with her finger. "If you have an early morning meeting with a female at a time when the male hormone is most active, I guess we'd better have a little pillow talk tonight ... just in case."

The law offices of Foster, Melham & Porter were located in One Shell Square on the corner of Poydras and St. Charles. The firm had nearly a complete floor, that alone testifying to their size and wealth. The offices were located in an impressive high rise on the "Miracle Mile," as that section of Poydras in known. Charles Porter met them at the reception desk. A portly man, in his sixties, bald, and overweight, he smiled a warm smile. "Mrs. Martin, good morning. Your sister spoke of you to me on several occasions, and may I take this opportunity to add to the condolences I extended the other day on the phone on behalf of the firm," and he looked at the plainclothed officer with her, asking, "And you, sir, are ... ?"

Mike extended his hand. "Sergeant Mike Fortier of the NOPD, Mr. Porter."

The attorney made no attempt to hide his surprise and displeasure. "Oh, I was not aware that Mrs. Martin's visit required police involvement, Sergeant. May I inquire why?" as he escorted them into a corridor.

The sergeant, following them, replied, "Her visit is not a police matter, Mr. Porter, per se, but when I visited Mrs. Martin on Monday of this week near Golden Meadow, she informed me that she would be meeting with you today. I insisted on being with her during this meeting because we at the department have reason to believe that the Swiss bank account her late sister had might have some bearing on this case."

As they entered his personal office and he showed Mrs. Martin to a chair, the attorney turned to the officer. "I'm not sure I approve of this, Sergeant. You do know there is such a thing as attorney-client privilege, and I might wish to exercise that in this case," and he waved the policeman to a chair.

Mike expected this from the attorney, replying, "I asked Mrs. Martin if you were her attorney and she replied, "No." Nedra was nodding her head in agreement. "So, you see, Mr. Porter, the attorney-client relationship does not exist between you two, and you certainly would not presume to make it retroactive, would you?"

The attorney smiled. "Of course not," and turning to the woman, asked, "Is that all right with you, Mrs. Martin, that the Sergeant be present during this meeting?"

She nervously looked from one man to the other. "I have no objection to his being here. I want him here."

"Very well, now that that is settled, we can proceed. Did you bring the plastic card with you that your sister had in the bank box?"

She nodded, removing it from her purse and handing it to the attorney. He read the number and the bank name, and then, excused himself to call the Swiss bank to see what he had to do to get account information. "They have a large branch in New York, and I'll place a call to them." A secretary came in with coffee and Danish rolls. He pointed to the tray as he picked up the phone. "Please, help yourselves."

As Mike poured himself and Nedra some coffee, the attorney began to talk to the New York branch. They could only hear Porter's portion of the conversation, but there was no doubt he was running into some trouble getting information on the account. They heard him protest, argue, plead, and then he hung up the phone, saying, "It is not going to be as fast as I had hoped. These Swiss bank accounts are based on secrecy, and they don't divulge the information in cases like this except on receipt of a notarized death certificate. "Mrs. Martin, do you happen to have a copy of the death certificate with you?"

Her eyes widened. "Oh, no. I had no idea ... "

The sergeant patted her hand. "Don't fret. Did the funeral home give you one, yet?"

She shook her head. "No. I don't have one."

The sergeant and the attorney exchanged glances, with the attorney saying, "I can send someone over to the bureau of Vital Statistics and see if we can put this on fast track. We know people over there, but it may take police intervention, Sergeant. Can you folks help?"

The policeman rose. "Yes, let me call the station and I'll have someone get on it. We may need to have a state judge get on this thing right away."

"I have another appointment for eleven. I'll have to turn Mrs. Martin over to you during that time, Sergeant. Any problem? Of course, she is perfectly welcome to sit in our reception room and read, or ... "

The policeman looked at the distraught woman and replied, "No, I know a sweet little housewife who will take good care of her until this afternoon, including a good lunch," and taking the woman by the arm, "Come on, Mrs. Martin, you and I are going to my house."

Protesting, she said, "Oh, I don't want to bother anyone. I'll just sit in the waiting room. I'll read some magazines. I'll be all right."

"But what will you do for lunch?" asked the sergeant.

The attorney replied, "No, problem. We'll take care of that. The secretaries order 'take-out' every day. We'll see that she is fed. You go about your business, Sergeant. Let's agree to meet here at one-thirty, OK?"

Rising to leave, he nodded, telling Nedra "Don't worry, you'll be all right. I'll see you at one-thirty," and turning to the attorney, "I'll see if I can't break the death certificate loose down at the Bureau," and he was gone.

Summary Justice

At one-thirty five he entered the offices of the law firm with a copy of Debra Barre's death certificate in hand. He walked up to the sister, attempting to hand it to her, but she turned away from it, as if it could do her harm. He said nothing in reply, understanding her feelings. The attorney came out, waving them into the corridor to his office. As they sat down, he went to his desk and after shuffling some papers, aimlessly, he shrugged his shoulders, saying, "While you were gone I had some time to spend on this thing, talking to the bank branch in New York. They, in turn, got on the phone to Zurich, trying to get authority to tell us what we want to know, which is what is in that account. The Swiss don't trust anyone in these matters. We had to call a law firm in New York, with whom we do business, and with whom they do business, to verify that we are who we say we are. Well, at least now they know who we are, and as soon as we fax them copies of the death certificate and the will, they will disclose the amount in the account. I had to convince them it is a police matter." He laughed. "I don't think they are ready to send us the cash today, but they will give us the balance." And turning to the policeman, he asked, "Will that satisfy you, Sergeant?"

He nodded. "For the time being, Mr. Porter. We will insist that no money be touched until the courts decide whose money it is."

The woman, hearing that, exclaimed, "Oh, I don't want the money. I'm scared to death of this. I don't want it."

The attorney smiled at her. "Now, Mrs. Martin, please don't make rash statements at this time. It will do no good anyway! Neither the sergeant nor I have the authority to decide who gets what. My responsibility is to carry out the provisions of your sister's will," and he added, "of course, within the bounds of the law, since this has now become a capital case."

Mike Fortier added, "And my responsibility, Mrs. Martin, is to see that if any laws have been broken the guilty must be charged. Then, it's strictly a legal matter, out of my hands."

Porter picked up a copy of the dead woman's will from his desk. He looked at the sister first, then at the policeman, asking, "I'm sure you will insist on being present during the reading of the will, Sergeant. I'm not quite sure you have that legal right at this time, but I have no objections if Mrs. Martin does not," and he looked at her.

She seemed confused, but she shook her head. "No, I don't mind if he stays in the room. I have no idea what it will say except what Debbie said in her note."

The attorney quickly read through the short and concise document. As promised, she left everything to her sister, Nedra Martin, with the proviso that her mother would be cared for until her death, and then the will

95

took a strange turn. If the sister, Nedra Martin, should precede her in death, then, her estate would be given to the Catholic Church, with only a small amount going to the children of Nedra Martin for their education. The policeman watched the woman as that provision was read. She twinged a noticeable amount. The only conclusion the policeman could reach was that Debra Barre' did not care for her brother-in-law, Oscar Martin.

The will having been read, the attorney called in a secretary to whom he dictated instructions for faxing the necessary documents to the New York branch of the Swiss bank listed on the dead woman's card. Then the attorney explained to both the sergeant and the sister the procedures which would have to be followed in carrying out the dead woman's wishes with regard to her estate. Mike Fortier hated having to spend the greater part of a whole day on this one matter, but he instinctively felt it would prove to be important enough to justify the time.

After nearly a half hour, the phone buzzed and the attorney picked it up. "Yes, this is Charles Porter, Mr. Heinman. Yes, I will repeat the number one more time for your benefit. Yes. Would you repeat that, please?" as his eyebrows went up, and he looked at both Nedra and Mike, he continued, "Yes, thank you. I'll inform her sister of that. Thank you, goodbye."

He replaced the receiver on it's base as he turned to the sister. "Mrs. Martin, your sister had a rather large sum of money in that account. Quite frankly, I'm amazed. I have been her attorney for two years and felt that I knew of her circumstances, but this exceeds my expectations, I assure you." He took a deep breath. "That account balance of this date, including interest is, two million one hundred seventy thousand U.S. dollars, and," he took a deep breath, "it is all yours ... if the courts agree."

She gasped and put her hands to her throat. "Oh, my God, Mr. Porter, where could a young woman like Debbie get her hands on that kind of money?" and she turned from the attorney to the policeman, to anyone, for answers. Mike Fortier could not suppress pursing his lips and blowing out air, for the amount staggered him. He had expected, maybe, another fifty thousand or so, at most, but two million one hundred and seventy thousand dollars far exceeded anything he had dreamed of.

The attorney, trying to bring the meeting to some semblance of reality after the hearing of that sum of money, said in his best legal demeanor, "Of course, Mrs. Martin, I hope you realize that this money will have to work its way through the courts. I must be candid with you and tell you that you may never get it if it was come by," and he lowered his voice, "illegal means."

The sister raised her hands in futility. "How else could it have been

Summary Justice

obtained? How could she have made that kind of money by legal means? I'm no fool, Mr. Porter. I know better than that."

Porter rose, signifying that the meeting was over, and after saying good-bye to them both, he pulled the sergeant aside, with, "What do you want me to do about this?"

He shook his head. "I don't know, yet. This is over my head. I'll talk to our legal department, but I know one thing; that lady is a long way from getting her hands on that money."

The attorney nodded. "I agree, but where the hell did Debra Barre' get that kind of money?"

He put his hand on the attorney's arm. "Mr. Porter, when I know that, I think I will have solved the case. Good-bye, and thank you. I'll see that Mrs. Martin gets home safely."

As he escorted her back to his car for the return trip to the Airport Hilton and her car, he took her by the arm as they sat in his car. He looked into her eyes, deeply and seriously. "Mrs. Martin, I am advising you as strong as I can, *don't breathe a word of this to anyone, no one, do you understand?*" and as those words sunk in, he added, "Your life may depend on it."

She began to cry, shuddering as she said over again and again, "Oh, my God ... oh, my God."

He looked at her with compassion, realizing she was in no condition to drive home. She would never make it, she was so traumatized. He drove instead to the precinct station house, and after a conversation with the captain, two police officers, one female officer and one male, drove her to the Hilton. The male officer got into Mrs. Martin's car to drive it back to Golden Meadow; the female officer, about her age, got into the police car with Mrs. Martin, who crawled into the back seat and assumed a fetal position. She stayed there until the policewoman looked back, some hour and a half later and said, "You're home, Mrs. Martin. Come on, I'll help you in, honey." Still as if in a trance, the woman pliantly allowed herself to be half carried to her home and into her bed by the two police officers.

Alcide Guilbert and Mike Fortier could hardly wait to see one another that evening, so great was the news each had to tell the other. Mike had rushed over as soon as he felt *The Wheel* was over, hoping to get his uncle's full attention, but as he pulled into the driveway he could see Rosalie's car parked farther in, toward the rear. She had always done that, parked her car far to the rear as if to fool the neighbors. He hesitated, not knowing if he should intrude or not. He thought to himself, " Who knows what they might be doing at their ages, in the twilight years of their lives." His dilemma was solved when he saw Rosalie coming out the front door, beaming, followed by a smiling Alcide Guilbert. Seeing Mike, she paused, saying loud enough for him and the neighbors to hear, "I hope you enjoy those white beans, Alcide, and that salt pork, too. I had to look all over town for that. It's hard to come by these days," then, "Oh, hello Michael, your uncle and I were just talking about you. How are Cindy and the kids? Well, I got to go. Bye, Alcide. Good to see you, Michael."

He smiled as he let her by, waiting for her to back her car out so he could drive his in. His uncle was waiting for him on the porch, still smiling, and as his nephew brushed by him with a smile on his face and raised eyebrows, the uncle grinned, saying, "Man does not live by white beans alone, you know," and turning into the house, asked the nephew, "What d'ya have?"

The nephew went directly to the fridge, extracted a Dixie and unscrewed the top, replying, "Unck, wait until you hear what I have. It'll blow your stack, believe me!"

The old man grinned. "Well, Michael the Archangel, I had a pretty good day, myself, but you go first," and as the younger man related the happenings in the attorney's office, the uncle listened with exclamations of, "No shit!" and "Sacre Merde."

When the young man had finished, the older man shook his head. "Poor woman. I'm not sure she can handle this. She is not too sophisticated, not like her little sister, Debra, for sure. As he rose to fill his pipe, he added, "Mike, we have got ourselves a real gasket buster, here, but it's beginning to make sense, a little, anyway. Let me tell you what I found out about the drilling venture," and he related the conversations with the disgruntled partners, and finishing, asked, "What do you think of that? It seems our boy, Marcel, and our girl, Debra, had themselves more trouble than they could handle. Marcel Gervais, for sure."

"But," rebutted the nephew, "we have not tied the thing together. I don't see the connection, yet."

The uncle puffed on his pipe. "No, I don't either, but you can bet your sweet ass there is one and a high voltage one, too."

"But Jo-Jo—how the hell does he fit into this mess?"

"I don't know, yet, but he does. All three of them offended someone—someone pretty damn powerful, too."

"Do you think it is local?"

"No! The local Mafioso would never have taken out Jo-Jo while the old man is still in charge, which he is, even though he maintains he is just a produce importer. No, it came from up above."

"But why?"

"That, my boy, is what we're supposed to find out."

The nephew looked downcast as he continued, "You know, Unck, the captain told me if we don't crack this thing in a week, he is calling in the FBI."

The old man chuckled. "I don't worry about what that dumb-ass says. He's always pulling that routine on the department."

"But, if he does, there goes my promotion."

"Well, my boy, we'll just have to see how it turns out. Tomorrow, I want us to go to Marcel Gervais's office. I'll bet there are some secrets there, if we can find them. Call your friend, Mr. Stern, and set it up."

"What do you hope to find there?"

"I'm not sure, but I want to look into this Esperante thing. I have a hunch that that project might give us the crack we need to put the crowbar in and pop this thing."

"I'll call Mr. Stern first thing in the morning after I get to the office. Do you prefer morning or afternoon, assuming we have a choice?"

The old man rose, stretched, and emptied his pipe in an old glass ashtray with a beer advertisement on its face. "Morning, if you can, I have many other things I want to do tomorrow, including having a talk with your boss and my old nemesis, the captain."

"What do you want to see him about?"

"The terms of my employment. I want to know how much authority I have in this matter, how much money I can spend, and so forth."

Not sure he understood, Mike replied, "Uh huh, I see," and rising, "I think I'll turn in, Unck. It's been a hard day and I've still got some work to do before bedtime."

The uncle reached for the remote control. "Yeah, goodnight, Mike. See 'ya in the morning."

The offices of Gervais & Stern, Architect/Engineers was furnished in the 1950-60 styles of black leather and chrome Herman Miller furniture trimmed with oil-rubbed walnut for added warmth. It was furnished in the style of the 50-60s because it had been there since then. Neither Marcel Gervais nor Irving Stern had seen fit to change it. Even when they had moved into this new building two years before they still held on to the old stuff with Irving Stern admonishing his spendthrift partner, "Marcel, let's be practical. They don't make furniture like this anymore."

The office had grown over the years and had a permanent staff of twenty-three on the engineering side, not counting the field crews who did the site surveying. The architectural side, since architecture is a feast or famine business, depending on the national economy and the public's propensity for spending money, varied from thirty to fifty people. A fairly permanent staff of twelve registered architects formed the nucleus of the design group, with drafting people taken aboard as needed. The accounting, though, was handled in one office, as was the billing for both disciplines, and the lady in charge of that department as she had been for over twenty-five years was Gloria Sanchez, a spinster by choice.

The receptionist, an attractive young woman of twenty-something, smiled as she saw the two men coming into the waiting room. She had been chosen for her looks, her warm personality and her well-modulated voice. As Marcel Gervais had told his partner, "First impressions are lasting ones, Irving. I've read in some executive magazine that the impression one gets when one first enters a reception room helps formulate the permanent impression of that firm." The more conservative partner grunted, "Then, Marcel, you're telling me that style is more important than substance," to which the late partner replied, "Exactly, Irving, especially in architecture."

Irving Stern, upon being notified of the two police officers' arrival, came to the reception room to fetch them. He managed a tight smile, as was his custom, with, "Ah, good morning, Sergeant. It is good to see you again," and turning to the uncle, "This must be Alcide Guilbert, the renown inspector of whom I have read much in the past." As he pointed them in a direction, he added, "I thought you had retired, Inspector Guilbert. Didn't they give you the gold watch treatment a few years back?"

Making his way down the corridor, the old inspector replied, "Yes, they did, but you know how it is, Mr. Stern, when a man punches the clock for forty years or more, it is difficult to quit," and he grinned as he added, "you know what they say about retirement: it is no fun because you don't get days off anymore."

The engineer smiled. "How true," he said, arriving at his office door. He waved them in, asking, "Would you gentlemen like some coffee?"

Mike shook his head. "No, thank you," while the coffee-fiend uncle answered, "Yes, I would, if it isn't too much trouble."

"No trouble at all," and punching the intercom, "Alice, would you please bring in a coffee for two. Yes, cream and sugar, too." From the uncle, "Sweet 'n' Low, please." The engineer nodded, correcting the instructions.

Irving Stern sat at his desk, glancing from one man to the other, then, "How may I help you, gentlemen? I think I've told Sergeant Fortier all I know about this unfortunate affair, but ... " and he raised his hands, smiling.

It was the uncle who responded. "Mr. Stern, we would like to find out about the Esperante project, everything about it, including the financial end of it," and he added, "especially the financial end of it."

Summary Justice

The engineer, seeing the young woman come with the coffee, replied, "Very well, as soon as we have our coffee, we'll go across the hall to the architectural section. I'll introduce you to Gloria Sanchez, who can give you all the financial data you wish, or," and he smiled, "all we have anyway." Turning to the younger man, he asked, "Are you sure you won't have some coffee, Sergeant?" and pointing to his cup, "This is my second and last cup for the day ... ulcers you know."

Mike shook his head. "No, thank you, I'm fine with this glass of water."

They crossed over to the architectural section, walking through the same waiting and reception room the two entities shared. As they walked through, Irving Stern nodded to the congregation of salesmen, contractors, and subcontractors who usually make up the humanity in a design office's waiting room. They walked into a large room with dozens of drafting tables—some occupied and others empty. He waved around the room. "This is our bull pen. We have a similar room on the engineering side. It's where most of the drafting gets done. He waved around the perimeter which was comprised of glass-walled cubicles, adding, "The project architects and the designers are located in those cubicles in order to give them some degree of privacy for their creative juices to flow unimpeded by distraction."

Mike whistled. "Whew, we're looking at a good-size payroll in this room."

The engineer nodded. "How true. We have to keep the work coming in so we can support an organization of this size. Sometimes the architectural side supports the engineering side, and sometimes vice versa."

The uncle inquired, "What is the legal entity of this organization?"

"We are a professional corporation. We issued stock just like any other commercial corporation."

"Who owns what in what proportion?"

"We each owned half, Marcel and I, just as our fathers did before us," and entering an enclosed room of some size, perhaps thirty by thirty, he paused at the door. "And this is the Esperante room."

The two officers entered, looking around the room whose walls were covered with drawings, perspectives, site plans, and charts. A large table in the middle of the room held various small-scale models of projects, some detailed and some in block form. Around the table were eight drafting tables covered with sheets of drafting paper and pencils, as if the people had gone to lunch and not come back. The men looked around, then Mike turned to Irving Stein. "But, it's empty! There's no one working on the project."

101

The engineer nodded, sadly. "I know. What else could I do after Marcel's death? I don't know where we stand on this project, so I shut it down until some determination is made. I have to check with the partners. You will recall ... or, did I tell you that this was a limited partnership deal, and that Marcel was the general partner?"

Mike nodded. "I think you made some reference to it, but not in detail."

"That's probably because I don't know the details. I told you that this was Marcel's baby ... he handled it all until the time at which engineering would be required, and then I would come into it."

"But," the uncle averred, "there must have been someone else in authority on this project," and waving his hand around the walls crowded with drawings, "Marcel Gervais could not have done all this alone."

"Oh, no," the engineer retorted, "I hope I haven't given you that impression. No, this project had a sizable staff working on it until ... " and his voice trailed off.

The uncle inquired, "Could we talk to the person next to Mr. Gervais in authority on this project?"

"Why, of course. That would be Justin Foreman. He was the architect working directly under Marcel; most capable and talented designer. I moved him back to his old office after the accident. Please wait here a minute and I'll get him," and he rushed out.

CHAPTER TEN

Mr. Stern located the architect who had captained the design team working on the Esperante project, Marcel Gervais' chief assistant. The two policemen began to walk around the room, perusing the myriad of drawings lining the walls. They would pause at one which caught their attention, then at another, saying nothing, then the nephew, "I admit I don't know doodly squat about architecture but some of this stuff is very impressive ... beautiful, really," he added.

The uncle continued to walk. "Uh, huh ... hum'mm."

The engineer returned, followed by a tall, thin man, forty something, with a bow tie, button down collar, and pleated trousers. If the police pair had known who Phillip Johnson was, and being untutored in the field of architecture, they did not, they would have said he looked like a young Phillip Johnson. That would have pleased the young architect for that was what he wanted to look like. He had a shirt pocket filled with pens and pencils of various sizes, shapes, and colors. The engineer brought him forward, presenting him to the officers.

"Gentlemen, I'd like you to meet Marcel Gervais' right hand man, Justin Foreman. Justin, this is Sergeant Mike Fortier," pointing to the nephew, "and this distinguished gentleman is Inspector Alcide Guilbert, both of the New Orleans Police Department."

The architect shook hands with both men. "Mr. Stern tells me that you want to be brought up to date on the Esperante project."

The nephew asked, "Are you able to tell us everything about it ... in detail?"

Walking to the table where the models were displayed, he replied, "If I can't, now that Mr. Gervais is gone, I don't know who could," and he pointed to one of the models, adding, "This layout here was to be the final design if we had the go ahead to proceed."

The uncle moved forward to examine the model. "What do you mean, 'If you had the go ahead to proceed'? I thought this project was in progress, a sure thing."

The architect shook his head. "Well, it was and it wasn't," and seeing the curious looks on the faces of all three men, he continued, "we had gone about as far as we could go without a definite site to work with, and as of today, we don't have one."

It was Irving Stern who interjected, "But, Justin, I thought the Rigolets site was just about jelled."

"No, Irving, it was not. As you know, we were looking at three sites for the project. Marcel's first preference was on the north shore of the lake, near Mandeville. The people from New Orleans could use the causeway to get to it, and the people coming in from Mississippi and the rest of Louisiana could use I-10, and the people coming in from the north could have used I-55. It was the best place, no doubt, but we ran into such stiff opposition from the locals and the environmentalists." He shook his head. "It was deemed unworkable. The next preference was the Bay St. Louis area, but we ran afoul of the Mississippi interests who were pushing their own casino projects, so the Rigolets area was our third choice, but we ran into big problems there, too."

"In other words," the uncle inquired, "the project had really run into a dead end."

The architect nodded. "It really had. As you know, the city was committed to one large land-based casino in the empty Rivergate, and the Levee Board was looking at allowing a floating casino on the south shore of the lake, so we had casinos coming out of our ears. Even Baton Rouge was looking into one tied up to a wharf near Catfish Town," and raising his hands, "How many casinos can one area accept and make a profit?"

The uncle asked, "Is this why the Canadian banks turned cold on the deal? They backed out, did they not?"

He nodded, as Irving Stern moved forward to hear the answer, proving his contention that he didn't know what was going on with this particular project, with the architect answering, "Yes, when they ascertained that we had big problems in even finding a likely site, and it became politically embroiled, they lost interest in the project and backed out..."

"But," asked Mike, "didn't you find some other financing?"

"Yes, Marcel did. I don't know the details because my job is design, not finance, but he made some trips to Florida and came back and told me he had located some funds there."

The two policemen exchanged glances with the uncle asking, "Did he say who, what bank?"

"No, he really didn't, not as I can remember. He did say something about the Cayman Islands, I remember that. He came back from one trip in a good mood, telling me, 'Justin, my boy, we're back in business. These people have guaranteed me that they will finance the project, and I have come back with a five million dollar letter of credit on a Cayman bank for our design fee money.'" The architect looked at all three men. "That's how I heard about the Cayman bank ... from that conversation."

Irving Stern moved forward, pointing his finger at the architect. "Let me get this straight, Justin. Marcel told you he had a five million dollar letter of credit for our fees on this project ... "

He seemed perplexed. "Of course, Irving, didn't you know?"

The engineer avoided the question. "Did he make any draws on that letter of credit?"

He shrugged his shoulders. "Well, I don't handle the books, as you know, but I have to assume he did," and he gestured around the room, "Look how much has been done on it, and," he smiled, "we all got paid, each and every Friday, just like clockwork."

"How much has been drawn on that account?" asked the engineer, obviously growing more curious all the time.

"I don't know, Irving. You'll have to ask Gloria Sanchez about that, but I know for sure some advances were made, because Marcel would say, jokingly, 'Well, we're still alive, Justin'."

The engineer seemed provoked as he exclaimed, "That is just what I intend to do," and turning to the two policemen, "Gentlemen, if you are finished here, please come with me to the accounting office of this firm. I am as curious as you are to know what is going on," and he stormed out, in sharp contrast to the low-keyed person Mike had first met. The two policemen, exchanging glances and, with raised eyebrows, followed him out, after a quick handshake with the perplexed architect.

Without knocking at the door of the head bookkeeper, Gloria Sanchez, he stormed in, followed by the two policemen. The bookkeeper, surprised at the swift intrusion of three men into her domain, looked at her employer with surprise.

"Oh, good morning, Mr. Stern, is there something I can get for you?" inquisitively glancing at the two policemen.

The engineer, in a calmer voice, now, "Yes, Miss Sanchez, you can get me the financial file on the Esperante project—all of it, please!"

With complete dismay, she replied, "But I don't have it, Mr. Stern."

He raised his voice. "What do you mean, you don't have it? Where is it?"

Her hands began to rub against each other and her lips quivered a little. She had never seen Irving Stern excited, before, ever, and she didn't like it. Nervously, she replied, "Mr. Gervais moved the files from my office three months ago."

"To where? Do you know?" he demanded.

"Well, I'm not sure, sir, but I think he put them in his office, in his personal filing cabinet." She added after a pause, "The reason I know is ... one day I needed some amounts to put in my books for accounting purposes and when I went to ask him, well, he kind of gave me a dirty look, and went to his locked filing cabinet and shuffled through the file. I recognized it and he gave me an amount of money I had to use for my books."

The engineer had calmed down and he was his old self, precise and pragmatic. "Miss Sanchez, do you have any knowledge as to how much money has been drawn on this project?" he asked.

She seemed almost afraid to answer, but replied, "He told me it was not the affair of the firm since the money was loaned to the partnership, and that our interest only involved the fees due the firm for work performed."

"Well, that is true, but we just looked at all the preliminary drawings on the project and in my professional opinion, all that work could not have come to one hundred thousand dollars. Do you have any idea how much money he had drawn so far?" She was almost in tears. "I don't know, sir. Mr. Gervais had set up a separate account on the limited partnership and he had the checkbook and he wrote the checks. I would present a bill to him for time spent by our people and he would give me a check for that amount." She began to sob. He put his arm around her shoulders. "Now, now, Miss Sanchez, we are not accusing or blaming you for anything," and he looked to the officers for support. They felt they had to nod in agreement, so they did, as the engineer continued, "We're just trying to get at the facts in this matter, that's all. Do you happen to have a key to Mr. Gervais's personal file cabinet?"

"Oh, no, Sir, he was the only one who had that. I have no idea where he kept it."

Turning to the two officers, the engineer said, "Please follow me, gentlemen. It is time we get to the bottom of all this," and turning to the still sobbing woman, inquired, "do we have a large screwdriver in this office?"

She looked up, surprised, "Yes, Sir, we keep some tools in the coffee room for emergencies."

"Thank you, Miss Sanchez. Now, please try to compose yourself. You have done nothing wrong, I assure you," and he waved the two officers on to the coffee room where he located a large screwdriver and a pair of vise-grip pliers, saying, "Please follow me, gentlemen."

As they entered the private office of Marcel Gervais, it was quite obvious that the two partner's different lifestyles carried over into their two different approaches to professional appearances. While the engineer's office had been sparsely furnished in basics, the architect's office could only be described as plush. Expensive furniture and art work were in evidence everywhere, from thick carpeting to wall-to-wall lined drapes that could be drawn by a remote control motor actuated by a servo unit. His large desk was made of Honduras Mahogany and inlaid with rare species of wood. In one corner of the huge office, the carpeting had been omitted and the flooring was of an inlaid tile, and that was where his drawing board was located, the tile being substituted for the carpeting where the debris produced by a drawing board erasure dust and shavings of pencils being sharpened would have ruined the expensive carpeting. At the other end of the room was a seating area for conferences. The two officers looked around, nodding to each other, suitably impressed. The engineer, slightly embarrassed, observed, "As I told you, before, Marcel and I lived different lifestyles," and as he waved around the room, added, "this was important to him while it would have meant nothing to me."

He went to a filing cabinet made of the same wood as the desk and the other furniture in the room, and turning to the men, shaking his head as if in despair. "I really hate myself for damaging this beautiful file cabinet, but I believe I must in order to get to the facts," and with that he inserted the long screwdriver in between the top drawer and the front of the unit. As soon as the screwdriver had enough leverage he applied the necessary force and popped it open, splintering the beautiful wood as he did. He looked at the two men as if to ask their concurrence as he leafed through the files, then grunting, "Ah, here is what we are looking for," as he extracted a file labeled: ESPERANTE PROJECT/LIMITED PARTNERSHIP. He carried the folder to the desk, followed by the two officers. He laid it on the desk and began to go through the contents. First, he extracted the legal papers which had formed the partnership, detailing the conditions of the agreement. It listed Marcel Gervais as the general partner, and then listed the limited partners. The two officers whistled as they reviewed the names, many of which were substantial people from many different locations in Louisiana, mostly people who had made big money in oil-related ventures, and were obviously eager to make more in the casino venture.

The uncle pointed to the list. "We'll want a copy of this entire file, Mr. Stern."

He nodded as he turned to what he really wanted, the financial section. He withdrew it, laying it on the desk so all parties could peruse it. He saw a copy of the letter of credit, just as the architect had stated, then, he began to see copies of the checks drawn on the credit line. He whistled as he passed them on to the officers, saying, "He has made some very substantial draws on this account," and as he used an adding machine on the desk, he added, "Very large draws, indeed." When he felt sure he had found all the payment requests, he totaled the tape, whistled, again, and passed it on to the officers, who in turn, also whistled. "Whew, this comes to two million dollars already drawn on the project," observed the uncle. "Does that seem reasonable, Mr. Stern?"

The engineer grunted. "Hell no, it does not. As I said, before, what we just witnessed, and it was all preliminary, would not in my professional opinion, amount to more than one hundred thousand dollars, at most."

"If that is so," opined the uncle, "then Marcel Gervais found someplace to spend about one million, nine hundred thousand dollars on something other than this project."

"That's a lot of money," observed the nephew.

"Yes," replied, the uncle, "enough to kill for."

The engineer seemed in a state of shock. "My God, this is a disaster for Marcel, and ... the firm, too, I'm sure."

The uncle nodded in agreement. "I must admit, Mr. Stern, it does not look good," he said, tapping the file on the desk. "This file tells us where and in what amounts the money came from, but I want to see where it went. He had to write checks to someone to get rid of that kind of money ..."

The nephew replied, proudly, "No, Unck, he might have spread it around in cash, you know."

"No, Mike, that won't do, unless he wants to have the IRS on his ass like flies on a dead carcass."

"What do you mean?"

"Anytime you deal in cash ... if you go to a bank with it, they have to report all transactions of ten thousand or more to the IRS."

"Well, he could have done it in smaller amounts, couldn't he?"

"Yes, he could have," and turning to the engineer still standing there in a state of shock, "Mr. Stern, where is the checkbook for this account?"

"I don't know. If it is not in that file, then he kept it someplace else. Let's have another look in the cabinet," and he pried open the other two drawers. "Ah, I think I see it in the bottom drawer. Yes, here it is," and he laid it on the desk as the two men crowded around, one on either side. As he flipped the cover open, it was obvious that the checks had been factory printed with the name "ESPERANTE LIMITED PARTNERSHIP" embossed on each check, with a background of a Mississippi steamboat sternwheeler under the printing.

"He meant for the checks to be impressive," said the uncle.

The engineer grunted. "That's the way Marcel did everything, impressively," and he added, somewhat sarcastically, "and expensively."

Running his finger down the checks, the uncle said in a low voice,

"There's his first deposit—a check for two hundred and fifty thousand, and he marked the stub ... retainage." He whistled. "That is a healthy retainage," and then his eyes widened as he thumped the checkbook with his forefinger, exclaiming in a loud voice, "Bingo! Look at this next check! Twenty-five thousand dollars, and look at who it is made out to...GOLDEN MEADOW RESOURCES," as he looked proudly at the other two men.

While the nephew smiled in agreement, the engineer said, "It means nothing to me ... does it to you? Who is Golden Meadow Resources?"

The uncle, grinning, replied, "I'm not positive, gentlemen, but I think we have just uncovered the first direct evidence of a tie-in between Marcel Gervais and Debra Barre', and I hope you can see that twenty-five thousand dollars is precisely ten percent of two hundred fifty thousand dollars."

The engineer slumped into the chair of his late partner, looking from man to man. "My God, what does this mean?"

"I'm not sure, yet," replied the uncle, "but do let us go on," and he ran his finger down the pages, saying, "uh-huh, and here is one to your firm, Mr. Stern, for six thousand, four hundred and twenty dollars ... for professional services, the stub says. I would imagine he is paying the firm for design and drafting services on the project, as Miss Sanchez said he did whenever she presented him with a bill from the firm."

The engineer nodded. "I would think so, yes, but the payments to Golden Meadow Resources? Could it have been for professional services? For land options? What?"

The policemen looked at each other, hardly able to suppress a grin. The uncle replied, "It is possible, of course, that these are legitimate payments to someone for services performed, but what kind of services, and more importantly, Mr. Stern, who is Golden Meadow Resources?"

"How do we find out?" asked the engineer.

Closing the book, the uncle replied, "Oh, I'm sure we can find out if it is a legitimate business. There will be papers filed in the office of the Secretary of State for the State of Louisiana, if it is a Louisiana business." He looked at the nephew, adding, "Of course, the name could mean nothing of substance, and the corporation, if it is one, could be registered in another state or," and he delayed for a moment, "or another country. Like the Bahamas or the Cayman Islands, for instance."

"How can we find out?" asked the perplexed engineer.

The uncle closed the checkbook, and turning to the engineer, said, "Mr. Stern, I feel that we have taken up enough of your time. I'm sure you want to get back to work and we need to move on, too." Picking up the checkbook and placing it under his arm, Alcide Guilbert said in official tone, "Mr. Stern, I wonder if you mind if we take this file and this checkbook with us as evidence in this case. I'm asking you informally but we can return with a court order if we have to."

The confused and perplexed engineer raised his hands in despair. "What difference does it make, now? This whole thing had turned to poopoo, has it not?"

The old detective nodded. "I think it has, Mr. Stern, but if it is any consolation to you, I don't see how the firm and you can be dragged into this. After all, the checks from the bank in the Caymans are made out to the Esperante Limited Partnership, not to the firm or to you."

He stood up, with his shoulders sagging, replying, "I will find very little consolation in that technicality, Inspector, I assure you. Now, if you don't need me anymore, I would like to get back to work. I have to consult with the firm's attorneys to see how we stand in this."

The inspector grabbed his arm, turning him around. "No, Mr. Stern, I'm afraid I can't allow you to do that! We have to keep this information under wraps for the time being. I hope you will cooperate with us ... voluntarily," he emphasized, strongly.

He seemed more confused than ever, and scared, as he twisted his hands in front of him. "Whatever you say, Inspector. I just want to do what is right."

"I know you do, and I assure you we will have all of our actions sanctioned by a judge—a court order—which will get you off the hook, so to speak."

"I would appreciate that."

As they walked to their cars in the parking garage, the nephew asked, "I didn't want to say anything in front of Mr. Stern, but why did you strong-arm him on the checkbook and file? The poor old man is scared to death ... "

"Michael, do you understand what we have uncovered here? If I am correct, this is the first hard evidence we've found of a link between Marcel Gervais and Debra Barre'. True," he continued as he slid in his seat on the passenger side, while the nephew slid into his, and he repeated, "true, that they died while being physically coupled in the act of copulation, to put it in genteel terms, but other than that, my boy, we have had no connection between those two people until now."

"But," asked a perplexed nephew, "supposing Golden Meadow Resources had nothing to do with Debra Barre', and it is just a coincidence—where are we then?"

He slid down in his seat. "Then, we're in deep yogurt, but I'll bet my right testicle against yours that such is not the case. Wanna bet?"

Summary Justice

The nephew groaned. "Hell, no! No bet! What now? Do you want to go to the station with that file and checkbook to place it in the evidence locker?"

He sat up. "Have you lost your mind? This stuff is staying with us until we crack this case. No, sir, Michael, it stays in our hands. Now, let's go to my house and pop the tops on a couple of Dixies and go over this stuff."

"Sounds good to me."

"Incidentally, keep this to yourself ... about the file and checkbook, I mean. Tell no one. It could get us killed if the wrong people in this town, or some other town, found out about this stuff."

"Shit, Unck, you think someone in *this* town is behind all these killings?"

"Could be, and then, it might not be. Michael, the way this world is these days, anyone can have anyone else killed at bargain basement prices." Rolling down the window and extracting his smelly pipe from his jacket, he began to stuff tobacco into it as he continued, "If I find the right dopehead badly in need of a fix, I can have someone killed for, maybe," and he flicked his Bic, "as little as fifty or a hundred dollars." He sucked on the pipe as the flame was drawn in, continuing, "Of course, that would be a sloppy job. You get what you pay for, and the dopehead would squeal on you as soon as he needed another fix and the police offered him one." Puffing and blowing a blast of smoke out the window, "But if I wanted a real pro job, I could go out on the international market and find someone who does that for a living, and they are good, too. Antiseptically clean—no prints, no evidence, no nothing. But they cost lots of money."

The nephew rolled down his window, taking a deep breath. "What's your point in all that philosophy?"

He smiled at the younger man. "My point is, these people have killed twice, and they would think nothing of killing again if it would protect their asses—that's my point. Now, let's get home. My hemorrhoids are bothering me."

He grinned. "What do you do for them?"

"Hell, don't you watch the TV commercials ... 'Preparation H', my boy ... temporary but blessed relief from," and he grinned, "the misery of the itching and swelling from hemorrhoids."

"Did you ever consider having them removed? They can do that, you know."

"Yeah, I know, but," and he slid down in his seat.

It took nearly an hour and three Dixies before they had thoroughly gone through Marcel Gervais's records, and as they finished, Alcide leaned back in his chair. "Michael, my boy, this thing is beginning to make sense to me. Does it to you?" Not waiting for an answer, he continued, "Everytime Marcel Gervais made a draw on that bank and made his deposit in the account of the partnership, the next check was in an amount of ten percent of his draw and it went to Golden Meadow Resources, but did you notice something interesting about that?"

The nephew sipped on his beer. "What do you mean?"

"Well, if you had checked the dates on the deposits and the checks to Golden Meadow Resources, you would have observed that it was never the same day, necessarily."

"Why does that matter?"

"Get me that calendar off the wall in the kitchen, will ya?"

Returning with the calendar, Mike asked, "What do you hope to find with this calendar, Unck?"

"Pay dirt," and as he compared the checks and the calendar, he said in a low voice, almost to himself, "now isn't that interesting?"

"What ... what ... dammit?"

"When you compare the dates of the checks with the days they met in the suite at the Royal Orleans, guess what?"

His eyes widened. "They matched?"

He nodded. "Just like clockwork, nephew. It seems that Marcel Gervais wrote a check to Debra Barre' for ten percent of his last draw on the day he was to meet her. How convenient! He didn't have to mail it. He didn't have to give her any large amounts of cash to attract the IRS by sending it on to a Swiss bank by way of a circuitous route. Hell," he mused as he sipped on his beer, "who knows how many times this money got laundered before it got to Zurich and into her secret account." He stood up and went to the mantel, filling his pipe and going through the whole Sherlock Holmes routine for the benefit of his wide-eyed nephew. "I don't know where that little girl from Lafourche Parish learned her finances, but she damn sure didn't learn it at LSU. No, sir, she got educated and sophisticated from a master, and it damn sure wasn't that dumb horse's ass Jo-Jo Terrafina, may his rotten soul rest in peace."

The nephew seemed perplexed as he stroked his chin, asking, "Do you think he paid her that kind of money for sex? That's pretty expensive stuff, don't you think?" and before the uncle could answer, he added, "hell, makes me tempted to go home and have a long serious talk with Cindy, tonight, if that is the going price, these days. I been out of the market for a few years, but, *whewee* ... "

"Don't be an asshole! That money wasn't for sex. It ain't never been worth that, even in times of long deprivation. No, that money was for ser-

Summary Justice

vices rendered out of bed, not in it." He relit his pipe, sucking on it as his head was obscured in smoke. "No, the sex was *lagniappe*' as we Cajuns refer to that little something extra the grocer used to give us as kids, but that was before your time," and as he waved his pipe in the air, "And it could be it was true love. Remember, her sister told us she loved an older man, and who fits that picture better than the handsome, debonair, dashing, bon vivant Marcel Gervais."

"So, you have it all figured out, huh?"

He shook his head and his pipe. "No! Not by a long shot! But, I am sure of one thing, though. Marcel Gervais was paying Debra Barre' a ten percent commission on every cent he drew on that Cayman bank. That's for sure!"

The nephew whistled. "That's a hell of a lot of money if she got a full ten percent on the whole two million he had already drawn. That's two hundred thousand dollars! Not bad for a little girl from Golden Meadow, down Bayou Lafourche."

The uncle scratched his chin in contemplation. "I'm glad you mentioned Golden Meadow. Something is bugging me about that name, and it is Golden Meadow Resources. We have to find out what it is and what it does. We need to find Debra Barre's files and records. Didn't you tell me that the department boys went over her apartment here in New Orleans with a fine tooth comb?"

"Yeah, the day after the killing."

"And, they found nothing of any interest?"

"No, I went over the stuff ... nothing."

"Humph! That's strange. If she handled that kind of money, she had to keep some kind of records ... somewhere."

"Maybe she was one of these people who could keep all that stuff in her head."

"No, she had to write checks, transfer money, that sort of thing. No, somewhere, she had a file. We just haven't found it, yet. As street smart as she was, it would have to be in a place she trusted, or, with someone she trusted, implicitly," and before he could finish the two men looked at each other and cried out, "Nedra Martin, her sister!"

The uncle stood up, excited, pacing the floor. "Yes, I'll bet you ten bucks that is where it is, in that house in her bedroom."

"But, I can't believe Mrs. Martin would have kept it from us, Unck ... "

"She didn't. She had no idea it was there, I'll bet. You remember we didn't give that room a close look out of respect for the dead, but, now ... "

The nephew smiled. "I guess we're going back to Golden Meadow, huh?"

113

"Yeah. I can taste the catfish already."
"I'll call her right now and see if we can go there tomorrow."

"But, of course, Sergeant Fortier, you and your uncle are welcomed to come, anytime, and this time the fried catfish are on me. You've been so good to me, I owe you something."

"Aw, you don't have to do that, Mrs. Martin ... "

The uncle who had gotten the drift of the conversation was kicking the nephew in the foot, shaking his head, forming the words with his lips—yes, yes!

"Well, Ok, Mrs. Martin, if you insist ... tomorrow," and hanging up the phone and turning to the uncle, "You got your home-cooked catfish."

FRIDAY MORNING

The nephew was solemn as he drove to his uncle's house, and his solemnity showed through as the older man climbed into the car. He gave the nephew a cheery, "Good morning, Michael. What a lovely day to drive down the bayou for some good catfish, huh?" And seeing the hounddog expression on the nephew's face, asked, "What's wrong with you? You and Cindy have a fight last night?"

He shook his head. "No, worse than that. The captain called me at home last night and told me that my week was up. You remember he gave me a week to crack this case and it is not cracked, so he is calling in the Feds". He started up the engine, adding, "The call upset me so much that I hardly slept, so I'm hung over, that's what is wrong."

"Is that so? Drive by the precinct before you head out. I want to have a talk with him ... man to man. You might have to take his crap, but I don't. He can suspend you, but he can't do a damn thing to me but run me out of his office and with all the stuff I've got on him, he won't try that."

"Oh, I don't know about that, Unck. You may be screwing up my career if you go in there and raise hell with him."

"Just do as I say, Mike! I knew Pat Monohan when he was a rookie cop. I helped him on a lot of cases when I was only a civilian consultant to the department. He owes his present position to me to a great extent. He couldn't find his ass with both hands if you turned him loose on his own, and he knows that I know that, too."

"Well, if you think so, OK, but I don't like this."
"Just do it!"

As they parked in the reserved space, the uncle got out, saying, "You wait here for me. I don't want you in the room when I explain the facts of life to Monohan."

"But ... "

"No buts, just wait here. I won't be five minutes."

The nephew kept looking at his watch. It had been over fifteen minutes since the inspector had gone in, and Mike felt sure something was wrong. But just as panic was about to take over, here they came, the uncle and the captain exiting the entrance door, with the captain's arm around the uncle's shoulders. "Now, A.J., you know I have the utmost confidence in you and Mike," and waving in the direction of the nephew, "Hi, Mike ... good morning. Well, A.J., I hope you have a fruitful day in Golden Meadow," he said, forcing a laugh. "You know we have a lot of heat on us on this thing—from city hall, the news media, even from Mrs. Gervais. Whew, that woman can turn on some heat in this town. You wouldn't believe it." And with a final pat on the shoulder, "Solve this baby, A.J."

The uncle nodded, "I'll do my best, Pat, you know that."

As they drove off, "What did he say? What did you say to him? He seemed to be in better mood."

The uncle laughed, "Well, I didn't have to say too much. We reminisced, mostly."

"You what? Reminisced?"

The uncle grinned. "Yes, I reminded him of the time I went looking for him and found him drunk in a Bourbon Street whorehouse, too drunk to go home to his wife, so I took him home and put him to bed, calling his wife and telling her that we had to go out of town on a case, and that he'd be home the next night. He said I saved his marriage." He chuckled as he slid down in the seat.

"Geez, is that what you guys talked about while I was stewing out in this car, worrying my ass off that they would take the case away from me?"

"Oh, he blustered about and said he could get us a few more days and all that crap, but if we don't produce in a few days, well ... " and he didn't finish.

"What'd you say about that?"

"I told him we'd have this case solved within a week, then he could call in anybody he wanted to. I don't give a damn."

"Do you think we'll crack it within a week?"

He sat up. "I don't know for sure what solving this case means to him or the media."

"What do you mean?"

He looked out the window at the passing scenery. "I think we'll find out who ordered the murders, but as far as catching the actual killer," and he shook his head, "I don't think we'll ever do that."

Lloyd J. Guillory

As he swerved to miss an eighteen wheeler, the nephew looked at the uncle with concern. "Well, do you think they will accept that?"

"Who?"

"The department ... the media ... City Hall ... the public?"

"What can they do about it, if we can't catch the killer? Will they sic the FBI on ... whom? Do you think the Feds are going to waste valuable manpower on a dead end? No. They'll ascertain that the killer is an international hit man and they will turn the thing over to Interpol and let it go."

"Do you think the killer was an international hit man?"

"I do, but I can't prove it, as yet. Perhaps we'll uncover something today that will reinforce my beliefs. I hope so, anyway," and he slid down in his seat.

She made a better appearance this day than on their initial visit and both men noticed it. Her hair had been done by a hairdresser, no doubt, and her dress was considerably more stylish than before. She had obviously spent some of her newfound wealth. She smiled, "Bienvenu ... welcome. Come in, please. I was hoping my husband would be home this time so you could meet him, but his boat sprung a leak and he had to pull it up at the shipyard. That boat! He thinks more of it than he does of me!" and she laughed a warm laugh.

As they entered the family room, they could see the tray with the cups and saucers, ready for the coffee, and the smell of fresh baked bread came from the oven. As she went to the kitchen to fetch the coffee, "It's only eleven o'clock, so I thought we'd have coffee and then you men can look for whatever you think it is you want in Debbie's room."

The nephew smiled. "That will be fine. I hope you didn't go to too much trouble with the food, today. We could have gone to the same restaurant. We enjoyed it last time."

She came back wearing an apron, and as she poured the coffee said, "No, I couldn't let you do that, Sergeant Fortier. You were too good to me when I went to New Orleans on Wednesday." She suppressed a sob. "I don't think I would have made it back without your help, I was so upset by all that bad news."

They noticed for the first time that she had a slight Cajun accent, indicative of having been brought up in a home in which the parents spoke French as their first language. It had been diluted with each generation, and was now hardly noticeable.

With genuine concern, the nephew asked, "And how are you doing now?"

She shrugged. "Better, although I still don't know what is going on. I can't imagine where Debbie got all that money," and she sniffed again. "It can't be legal, I know that."

In an attempt to appease her, the uncle replied, "Mrs. Martin, we still don't know that Debra has done anything legally wrong," and he placed emphasis on the word "legally".

"Oh, God, I hope not. It would kill Mama. Poor thing, I'm not sure she understands what has happened to Debbie, yet."

The uncle asked, "But, you did tell her, did you not?"

She wiped a tear with her apron. "Oh, yes, I had to, but she is half senile now, and I'm not sure she understood what happened. When I said, 'Mama, Debbie has died,' she looked at me so funny, and she said, 'No, my baby is not dead. She's gone to sleep that's all.' So I never argued with her, poor soul. Maybe it's better she doesn't understand. It's less painful that way," and Mrs. Martin touched the cross hanging from her neck, adding, "It's God's way."

She noticed that the men had emptied their cups. "Do you want more coffee? I have lots more on the stove."

The uncle rose, anxious to move on, "No, thank you. If it is all right with you, we'd like to see Debra's room once again."

She stood. "Of course. I haven't touched anything since you were here on Monday."

It was the uncle who asked, "Mrs. Martin, has anyone contacted you since we saw you last. Has anyone come to the house to ask you about Debra's things, anything like that?"

She looked surprised. "No, no one at all."

At the door to her sister's room, Nedra paused, as if reluctant to go in. "You don't need me, do you? I have some things on the stove. We can eat whenever you finish in here if you want to," and turning to leave, "I hope you're hungry."

They waved her off. "No, you go ahead and cook. We'll just be a minute in here," and watched her disappear down the corridor.

Mike flicked on the light switch near the door and several lights came on various table lamps around the room, flooding the bedroom with soft light. The smell of her fragrance was still in the air as they went to the dresser area. A bottle of expensive perfume was on the dressing table. Her makeup paraphernalia was still spread out on the tabletop as if she had gone out of the room for a moment and would be back in an instant. Her nightgown was still thrown across the bed as if a maid would be expected to retrieve it and place it in the closet. She had obviously bathed that morning and her soiled clothing had been left on a wicker basket in the bathroom, once again, as if a maid were expected to clean up. They concluded that Nedra Martin acted as her sister's maid.

The nephew fingered the underclothes as if they held some clues to her impending doom. He turned to the uncle, saying softly, "From what Mrs. Martin told us of her schedule, Debra spent each Wednesday night, every other week, here in this room. From what I see here, she would arise on Thursday morning, bathe, and dress in preparation for her afternoon liaison with Marcel Gervais."

The uncle nodded, then added philosophically, "Yes, like a bride going to her wedding couch. Poor girl. Shakespeare was right when he wrote, 'Oh what a tangled web we weave, when first we practice to deceive' ... how true, how true."

They began to open drawers, examine each nook and cranny of the room, but nothing was in evidence except that this was the bedroom of a lovely woman in the prime of her life. They looked for photographs of Marcel Gervais, but much to their surprise, found none but more to their surprise, they did find an oval frame of embossed silver, and therein was the photograph of a very handsome man, Latin-looking, about forty years old, with a full head of hair just beginning to gray at the temples. He was smiling a very warm and happy smile. The uncle picked up the photo for a better look, and turning to the nephew and pointing at the photo, "Handsome cuss, isn't he." And that damn sure is not Marcel Gervais."

The nephew closed in for a better look. "No, it isn't. Evidently, this girl had another man in her life. We have got to know who this man is," and he replaced the frame on the table. They looked at each other with the uncle saying, "We've checked everything in the room and have found nothing. I'm very disappointed, quite frankly," and turning to take one more look at the bed, and idea struck him, and he started to bend down to look under the bed, but the limitations of an arthritic back made him think twice about it as he said, "Mike, bend down and see if there is anything under the bed ... you never know."

The nephew gave him a knowing grin. "What would you do without me, old man. Wow, I see a bag, or something."

"Well, take it out. Let's have a look at it."

He extracted a medium-size traveling bag which obviously went to her complete set of luggage. He placed it on the bed and opened it. It was not locked. Inside, they found skirts, blouses, and sweaters neatly folded, and as Mike ran his finger in and among them, he blurted, "Oh, what have we here?" and he pulled out a briefcase covered with Moroccan leather—an expensive briefcase. It had a polished brass nameplate under the handle with the engraved letters: Debra Barre', and it had her sister's Golden Meadow address. He attempted to open it, but it was locked. The two men looked at each other, then the uncle said, "Open it, even if it means breaking the lock."

He looked around. "I don't have anything on me to break this lock. We'll have to get something from the kitchen."

"Just ask Mrs. Martin to come here with a screwdriver if you will. I think we should ask her if we can open it, and I want her to be present when we do. I want her to be a witness to whatever is in here."

He returned with her, as she wiped her hands on her apron, asking, "What's wrong? What did you find?"

The uncle pointed to the briefcase. "Mrs. Martin, have you ever seen this briefcase, before?"

She seemed surprised. "Oh, yes, I've seen it many times. Debra always had it with her when she came here. Where was it? I thought she had taken it with her when she left that morning to go back to New Orleans."

The uncle pointed to the bag resting on the bed. "No, it was in that bag under some clothing, as if she tried to hide it. Do you mind if we force it open? It is locked and we don't have a key. That is why we needed a screwdriver. Do you mind?"

She answered, nervously, as she wrung her hands, "I guess not. What difference does it make now?"

He replied, "That's how we see it, and we must check the contents," and he forced the lock, hearing it pop open on it's spring retainer. Looking inside, his eyes widened as he saw files and checkbooks. "Ah, Michael, we may have found what we were looking for," and as the nephew and the sister moved in, he asked the woman, "Mrs. Martin, before we get into this, would you tell us who the man is in that photograph on the dresser?"

She glanced at it for only a brief moment. "Oh, that is the man I told you about from Florida, Gino LaRoca. That was the man she was in love with when she lived there, remember?"

From the uncle, "Oh, yes, the man she loved but refused to marry because he was in the rackets, or something like that?"

She nodded. "Uh huh, that's the one."

"She evidently had some warm feelings for him if she kept his photo on her dresser."

The woman nodded, "Oh, yes, they remained good friends until she ... They talked on the phone nearly every week or so. She'd call him from here, or he'd call her, but it sounded like business to me, what little I heard. When he called and she took the call in the family room, she always talked on the portable and came into this bedroom. That's all I know."

"You've been very helpful, Mrs. Martin," said the uncle. And with a smile he asked, "is the catfish about ready?"

She seemed surprised. "Don't you want to go through the briefcase before you eat?"

Taking it in hand, he headed out the bedroom. "No, it can wait until we finish. I would like you to be present when we go through it and I know you are busy with the cooking and I want my nephew to watch you fry the fish. You see," as he led her out of the room by the elbow, "I've been trying to tell him how catfish should be cooked and ... "

As they entered the kitchen, he went to the counter where the fish nuggets were stored in a deep dish, already covered with batter. The uncle asked, "Do you make you own batter? What do you put in it?"

She blushed, "No, I don't make my own batter. I used to, but now I cheat like everyone else. There are so many good Cajun fish-fry batters on the market that it's just not worth the trouble anymore. I bought the Luzianne spicy, so I hope it is not too hot."

"No problem with me," replied the uncle, and taking the nephew by the elbow, "Come and see this. See how Nedra—may I call you Nedra since I am old enough to be your father?" And getting a smile and a nod, he continued, "See how she has cut the fillets into small pieces? That's the way to do it."

The nephew looked, with feigned interest. "Uh huh, I see."

They sat down to a Cajun lunch of fried fish, potato salad, sliced tomatoes fresh from the vine, fried onion rings, fresh baked French bread, and a Dixie beer in a frosty glass.

"Oh, mais bon Dieu, c'est bon, Madame, tres bon," cried the uncle in a language he felt he and the lady shared, while nodding to his monolingual nephew, "It's good, huh?"

The nephew replied, "You know, Unck, you're right about the frying of catfish, no doubt about it."

"And so many other things, Michael, too numerous to mention in front of this lady," and turning to their hostess, "Nedra, I can't remember when I have had a more enjoyable lunch, and in prettier company." She looked at the floor, blushing, for compliments were rare for her these days, as she replied, "I'm so glad you enjoyed it. I enjoy cooking for people who appreciate it."

The uncle stood. "Now, can we get on with our work?"

"Oh, but you haven't had your coffee. We always have coffee after our meals."

He patted his stomach. "Not for me, Nedra. I am full, but perhaps my nephew ... "

"No, thank you. I've had enough, too. Shall we have a look at the briefcase?" and they left for the family room where the briefcase was laid on the coffee table. The nephew slowly extracted the documents and handed them to his uncle as Nedra sat nearby, nervously fingering her apron. The first thing out was a Manila folder, which held a miscellaneous assortment of bills and letters, none in any order. She apparently threw them in as she received them. The uncle perused them, saying as he did, "Hummm ... that is interesting," and showing it to the sister, "Does this mean anything to you?" to which she generally responded by shaking her head. At last the checkbook was extracted, and as the nephew opened it, he smiled as he handed it to the uncle. The checks were printed with the words ... GOLDEN MEADOW RESOURCES, P.O. Box 897, GeorgeTown, Grand Cayman Island. The two men exchanged glances as the uncle showed the book to the sister, asking, "Have you ever seen this checkbook before, Nedra? Does this name, Golden Meadow Resources, mean anything to you?"

She looked from one man to the other. "Well, yes. I heard of the name before. I guess she named it after the town she was born in," and then taking another look at the checkbook, added, "she made out some checks to me from time to time on that account. That's how she paid for the addition to this house, and that is how she paid for my car, and she pays Mama's nursing home bills out of that account. Of course, she puts the money in a local bank in Golden Meadow and writes the local checks out of that," and she took a deep breath as she continued, "She had to because the local bankers gave her a hard time on those checks, at first, because they were on a foreign bank, so you know Debbie ... she said, 'To hell with them' and she would make a large deposit in the local bank with a cashier's check on that foreign bank."

The uncle's eyes widened as he saw several checks made out to Tideland Drilling. He turned them over and noticed that they had been deposited to that account in a New Orleans bank. He whistled. "Those checks made out to Tideland Drilling come to over two hundred thousand dollars. Isn't that interesting?" and turning to the sister, "Nedra, does the name 'Tideland Drilling' mean anything to you?"

She took a deep breath. "Not much. I believe I heard Debbie mention it one time, maybe two, when she was talking to Gino."

The uncle nodded. "Did you ever talk to him ... to Gino?"

"Oh, sure, many times, when he'd call for Debbie and I would answer the phone."

"What did he sound like?"

She shifted in her chair. "I don't know what you mean."

"Well," said the uncle, "you mentioned that he was in the rackets. You know how those people talk. You've seen them on TV and in the movies. Did he sound like he was from Brooklyn or the Irish Channel in

121

New Orleans ... you know what I mean, they say *dees* and *dem* and *does*," he smiled.

She became serious. "Oh, no, not Gino. He's a lawyer! He's a well educated man. He sounds like a college professor when he talks," and she hung her head down as she confessed, "I went to Nicholls for three semesters. I guess you can't tell that, now, but I quit to get married. I know I made a big mistake. I should have finished college. Look at Debbie, what she did with her life," and then she gave them a quizzical look, realizing that her dead sister might not have been a wise choice as a role model.

"Then," pressed the uncle, "you would have no idea why your sister would make out checks totaling over two hundred thousand dollars to Tideland Drilling."

"My God, no!"

He rose. "Nedra, my dear lady, we have taken up enough of your time and hospitality, and it is time for us to get back to the big city of New Orleans. How can we ever thank you for all the help you've given us?"

She blushed. "Oh, I didn't do much ... just fried a little fish for you that's all."

The uncle patted her shoulder. "No, my dear, you have done much more than that, believe me," and he patted the briefcase as he added, "I will be forced to take this briefcase with me. It has some very pertinent information in it that pertains to this case. If we run across anything that we feel should be yours, we will return it to you, I promise."

She shrugged her shoulders. "What difference does it make now?" More a statement than a question.

Driving along the bayou on their way back, the uncle was deep in thought. The nephew waited for him to make his usual philosophical treatise on their findings, and when he did not, the nephew asked, "Well, what do you think?"

He did not answer him before he took the pipe out of his pocket, stuffed it with Carter Hall pipe tobacco, and exposed it to the flame, while lowering the window for his nephew's sake, then finally, "Michael, this thing is beginning to make sense to me. Does it to you?" and he puffed hard, trying to make a reluctant pipe come to life.

The nephew nodded. "Yeah, I can see a little daylight, now. Marcel Gervais, for reasons not quite clear yet, had overdrawn on his five million dollar advance from the bank in the Caymans. He had paid Debra Barre' two hundred thousand dollars in commissions from that money and she, in turn, has given, or loaned, that same amount to Tideland Drilling, a venture controlled by Marcel Gervais, but as far as we know, she had no legal interest in. Am I hot, or just warm?"

The older man puffed, then grunted, "No, Michael, you are warm. In fact that's very good. If you were in my Detective 101 class, I would have to give you a 'B' on your deduction, so far."

He smiled, "No more than a 'B', Unck?"

"No, not for now, because the course is not over. You have not taken the final exam as yet, and I give tough finals."

"I guess you want to know why they were killed, huh?"

He looked at the nephew, grinning, "That's the only way we will get a passing grade from city hall and the public."

The nephew sighed a deep sigh. "I swear, Unck, I don't know where to go from here, except to dig deeper into the affairs of Marcel Gervais and Debra Barre'. Those two were up to more than a roll in the hay, believe me."

The uncle smiled with a satisfied look. "Did I not tell you this from the beginning? Did I not tell you it was not about sex?"

"You did, if that brings you any satisfaction. I'll admit you did, but ..."

"But what?"

"As I see it, Marcel Gervais could have done all this without the sex thing if money was the object to it all."

"Michael! Michael! Your strong middle-class morality and Jesuit High School exposure is blinding your perception of the real world. Did you see the pictures of Debra Barre'?"

"Yes, of course I did."

"And, was she not beautiful and desirable?"

"She damn sure was."

"Have you never heard of mixing business with pleasure?"

He grinned as he looked at the uncle. "Uh-huh, I sure have. Do you think it would do any good to go and have another talk with Mrs. Gervais?"

"For what purpose?"

"To see if she knows anything about Tideland Drilling."

Continuing to look out the window, watching the shrimp boats plying the bayou, "I doubt that she does, except in a peripheral way. You see, Michael, due to your economically deprived lifestyle, you don't understand the rich. If Marcel Gervais had ever mentioned the drilling venture to his wife, it would probably have been over brandy one night after dinner, and the conversation would have gone something like this: 'Elsbeth, love, I've been thinking of drilling for an oil well,' and she would have responded with, 'That's lovely, dear. What ever will you do with it if you find it?'"

Lloyd J. Guillory

The nephew looked over at the grinning uncle, "I guess you're right, Unck. That poor woman didn't know what the hell was going on. What do we do next?"

The uncle sat up, turning his gaze from the window to his nephew. "We now have both checkbooks in hand. Let's sit down and calmly and quietly, over a cool beer at my place, try to find some correlation between these two accounts. For instance, if Marcel writes Debra a check for 'x' amount of dollars, does she turn around and write a check of similar size to someone else for 'x' amount of dollars, and to whom. Get the picture?"

CHAPTER ELEVEN

FRIDAY NIGHT

At opposite ends of the same couch, the two checkbooks between them, and the Dixie beers at their sides, the two policemen settled down to an evening of "braining."

The uncle took the Gervais checkbook, turning the pages slowly. "Hummm ... hummm," he said.

The nephew, finding nothing special to "hummm" about, asked, "What? What?"

"This is most interesting, Michael. We, along with Irving Stern, have been wondering where Marcel Gervais had spent that two million that was supposed to be for design fees. Well, here are some answers. Here is a check for one hundred-fifty thousand dollars to the Mandeville Land Company, and one for two hundred thousand to the Bay Real Estate Co. in Bay St. Louis, and here are several to some organization called Coastal Real Estate for four hundred thousand. Whew! That is a lot of money, and obviously all for land or, as he listed on these stubs, "OPTIONS."

The nephew looked at the stubs with interest. "Those names would tie in with the locations that the architect, Justin Foreman, Marcel's right-hand man, gave us as the sites they were interested in. I guess he was trying to tie up these sites with option and purchase rights so he could move on the one he felt was most viable. Think so?"

Still perusing the book, "Uh-huh, makes sense as far as telling us where the money went, but from a business stand point, it makes no sense to spend money on three different sites when you can only use one of the three, unless ... "

"Unless what?"

"Unless, he did not plan on getting the money back from some of these people."

"That doesn't make any sense, Unck. What are you getting at?"

The uncle sipped his beer, stood up, and walked to the mantel, picking up one of his smelly pipes and going through the lighting routine.

"Michael, you know this gambling casino thing has been very controversial throughout the state, with the bible belt people fighting it like hell and the fun-loving Cajuns all for it—mostly, that is."

The nephew nodded.

"Then, there have been the Las Vegas and Atlantic City people fighting it on the basis that it is not in their best interest, which it isn't since there are just so many high rollers per square acre in this country and a large gambling casino in New Orleans will just dilute their share, since many high rollers came from Louisiana, especially during the oil boom, and they all know it will boom again some day," and he puffed on his pipe, "simply because it always does."

"I don't follow you. What's your point?"

"My point is that a lot of money has changed hands on this thing, and is still being changed every day."

"Are you trying to tell me that some of this money might be bribe money, that Marcel Gervais was actually bribing some of these people on the pretext of paying for land options he never planned to exercise?"

"I'm saying that it is a possibility, that's all. Nothing else makes sense. Marcel Gervais was too smart a man to pay that kind of option money on three sites at one time, unless he felt sure he would get it back some way or another. That's all I'm saying."

"How do we find out about this?"

"The simple way, at first glance, would be to see who owns these real estate companies, but I doubt that will do much good."

"Why? Seems logical to me."

He grunted. "Hell, Michael, we're not dealing with amateurs in this matter. There will be dummy corporations and blind names and every other trick in the book, and it will be like trying to find the end of a maze, with wrong turns here and there and everywhere."

Mike raised his hands questioningly. "Then, what'll we do?"

The old man sighed. "Hell, what can we do but try to find out who they are. Tomorrow morning, why don't you put some men on this, the courthouse boys who know how to go through the records. It wouldn't hurt to have a department attorney go with them. They know the ropes. If they're domestic corporations, we'll find out who did the incorporating, and if they're foreign ... well, at least, that will tell us something about the whole deal."

He rose to go. "Yeah, that it stinks."

The old inspector shook his head. "You know what bugs me more than anything else about this whole thing?"

Making his way to the door, the nephew looked back. "What?"

The old man followed his nephew to the door. "Marcel Gervais, that's what. Why did he get himself embroiled in something like this? Was it the career slide as Irving Stern thinks, or, was it something else?"

"I don't know, Unck, and I'm sure we won't find out tonight, so I'm going home to my wife and kids. I'll see you first thing in the morning. I guess we need to sit with the captain and maybe the chief, too, and tell them what we've got, and see what they want to do with this thing ... huh?"

"Yeah, I guess so. Goodnight, Mike."

The old inspector sat in his chair long after the nephew had left, mulling over the entire case. He would shake his head, take another tangent, explore another course. He had nearly dozed off when the telephone rang. He came awake, startled by its sharp ring near his ear. He looked at the clock on the mantle, which showed nearly ten thirty. He smiled, thinking it must be Rosalie. No one else would call him at this time of the night. She often did it when she couldn't sleep, cooing, "Alcide, I'm having trouble going to sleep. Why don't you come over. We could watch television for awhile, you know." He picked up the receiver, saying in a romantic voice, "Hellooo."

"That you, Alcide? Damn, you sound funny."

He sat up, wide awake. He knew that voice. "Is that you, Monohan? What the hell are you calling me for at this time of the night? I hope this is important..."

"It is, Alcide, I promise you."

"What, then? What?"

"I just got a call from the office a few minutes ago, and they said the FBI wanted me real bad, so I put the call in." He chuckled as he continued, *"I guess I woke the poor bastard up, too, because the call came from Miami, and its eleven thirty over there."*

"What did he want, Monohan? Get to the point, please."

"We've got a big break in the Gervais case, that's what. Some guy out there has asked for a plea bargain. He's a member of the Garaci family—You heard of them?—and he asked us to send out the man in charge of the Gervais case. He wants to talk. How about that?"

"Did you call Mike and tell him that? He is the officer in charge on this thing. You know that, Pat."

The voice sounded impatient. *"Aw, come on, Alcide. Cut out the bullshit. Are you trying to tell me that you are willing to suck hind titty to your nephew on this thing ... you, with all your seniority. Come on!"*

"You got it right, Pat. I'm the kid's assistant, and that's the way it's got to be, and that's the way I want you to play it. Now, goddammit, will you call Mike and tell him this, just like you never called me. Will you do that for me?"

There was silence for a moment, then, "All right, you grouchy old bastard, I'll do it on one condition."
"What's that?"
"They want us to fly out to talk to this man. Will you agree to go with Mike?"
He thought for a while. "Yeah, I promise, Pat. Do you know the name of this canary who is willing to do all the singing?"
"Yeah, they mentioned him. His name is LaRoca, Gino LaRoca. Mean anything to you?"
The old inspector smiled to himself. "Yeah, Pat. I've heard of him. Now, call my nephew, will you? Goodnight!"
As Alcide placed the receiver on the base, he sat down on the couch, smiling to no one in particular, saying, "Well, what do you know about that? Gino LaRoca! Bingo!"
He leaned back on the couch waiting for the phone to ring, knowing full well it would. It did, within five minutes, and an excited voice at the other end said, "Unck, guess what?"

Pat Monohan, the precinct captain, turned his gaze from Mike Fortier to Alcide Guilbert, asking, "Well, what do you think, men? Have we got something here, or not?"
Mike looked to the uncle for a reply, not sure what they had in the call from the FBI. The uncle thought for a moment. "We can't be sure, Pat, but if this means what I think it means, it will help us break the case. We know from our investigation of Miss Barre's past that these two people, at one time, shared a close, even an intimate, relationship. And, furthermore, according to the sister in Golden Meadow, they continued a friendly relationship, of sorts, until the end."
"Really? That is interesting. I guess this Mafioso family lawyer can tell us a lot about that broad."
The old inspector raised his hand in protest. "Please don't refer to the dead girl as a broad, Pat. She may have had some faults, but she came from a good, solid Cajun family down the bayou."
In a sneering voice, "Oh, yeah, don't get sanctimonious with me with all that sociology crap, Alcide. She was the mistress of Jo-Jo Terrafina, and that don't say much for her choice of men friends."
The uncle shook his head. "Our investigation has shown that such was not the case. I admit she was seen about town with Jo-Jo from time to time, but that could have been more of a business relationship than a love affair. As a matter of fact, the sister, Nedra Martin, who I believe is an honest woman, completely free of guile, told us in no uncertain terms that Miss Barre' did not love Jo-Jo. On the contrary, she could not stand

him, from a personal standpoint."

"Aw, what the hell are you talking about, Alcide?" and turning to the nephew, "Mike, I listened to that tape you made of Jo-Jo's little meeting with you the day after the murders, and didn't he say he loved the woman, and they were supposed to be married?"

The nephew nodded, "Yeah, Captain, but that was only his perception of it, and you know that little bastard would rather climb a tree and lie than stay on the ground and tell the truth. She was damn sure not in love with him! In fact, she was in love with Marcel Gervais."

"Geez! You just told me she was in love with this Gino ... what's his name? ... in Florida! How many men can one woman love at a time?"

The inspector smiled. "It depends, Pat, on her capacity for love. Some women have it in great amounts and others ... well, you know."

"Oh, geez, more sociology crap! Are you guys ready to travel? We have reservations for you out of Moisant at 2:15 this afternoon, and I hope to hell you come back with some answers to this mess, including Jo-Jo's death. Incidentally, do you think they are tied together—the two murders?"

The old inspector rose to go. "Like shoestrings, Patrick. Just like shoestrings. See you in a day or so," and turning at the door to look at the captain, smiling, "You do know I charge my full consulting fees even while I am traveling, plus all out of pocket expenses fully reimbursed."

The captain waved him off, smiling, "Aw, get the hell out of here, you old worn out reprobate."

As they made their way to the parking garage, the uncle joked, "Now, wasn't that a nice warm conversation we just had with the captain, Michael?"

"If I didn't know better, I'd swear you two guys didn't care for each other."

"Aw, we do! We just don't want the other to know it."

Reaching for the car door handle, the nephew asked, "Are you packed and ready to go, or do you have to go home, first?"

"No, I'm packed. I packed this morning just before I went to tell Rosalie good-bye."

The nephew smiled. "You went to tell Rosalie good-bye this morning?"

"Sure. Why not?"

"What time? We were in the captain's office by nine."

He seemed just a bit bashful, avoiding the nephew's gaze. "We had coffee at seven. She had coffee and biscuits ready for me when I got there."

"Oh, and how long did that take," the nephew asked, grinning.

"It doesn't take long to have coffee and two biscuits, Michael. You know that?"

"Yeah, I know! What did you do between that time and the time I picked you up at 8:45?"

"We said good-bye, of course," and he smiled, adding, "are you packed?"

"Yeah, my bags are in the trunk."

"But, aren't you going to go by the house and tell Cindy good-bye?"

Now, he looked embarrassed. "No, we said good-bye last night. How many good-byes can a man stand in so short a time?"

The uncle slid down in his seat, grinning, "It depends on a man's capacity for love."

As he hit the starter button, "Don't give me that sociological crap, Unck."

Neither man said much during the direct flight to Miami, each either dozing off or deep in his own thoughts, with each wondering what the trip would bring in the way of information. Just thirty minutes from Miami International, the flight attendant came down the isle, checking seat numbers, stopping at 18-A and 18-B. Looking at both men, asking, "Sergeant *For-teer*?" unsure of her pronunciation.

He smiled. "That's close, but *Fort-yea* is even closer."

She smiled, embarrassed, "I'm sorry. I'm not too good with French names," and then she blushed, "even though I went with a New Orleans Cajun for a while."

The old inspector could not resist, "You evidently did not go with him long enough, my dear."

She smiled. "Well, anyway, the captain has asked that you come to the flight deck. He has a message for you."

The nephew gave the uncle a quizzical look, shrugging his shoulders, then rising to follow the young lady to the front cabin. She unlocked the door to the pilot's compartment, leading him in, then to the pilot, "Captain, this is Sergeant *Fort-yea*," and she smiled as she backed out of the cabin, leaving the police officer alone with the two pilots. The captain gave his co-pilot a nod, then, "Sergeant, would you show me some ID, please?"

Not sure what he wanted, the sergeant nodded, extracted his police identification from his jacket pocket, and passed it to the pilot. The pilot, after perusing it, returned it, saying, "We have a message for you from the Miami office of the FBI. They had flight control call us and had us switch to a coded channel. The message is this: 'When you get to the airport, you will be met by two FBI agents who will be standing next to the

Delta counter at our gate, which is number 118, Concourse D. They will both be wearing dark blue suits, and they will have a man with them who will have a DEA jacket on. They say you can't miss them. One agent is six feet five and weighs two hundred and forty-five pounds, and looks like an NFL linebacker, the other is short and bald. Any questions?"

He smiled, "No, thanks, a blind man could find that group," and he backed out the flight deck area. The flight attendant was anxiously waiting outside the door, looking nervous, and asked in a confidential tone, "We're not being hijacked, are we?"

He smiled, "No, not today."

She shrugged, "You never know on this run. Can I get you two gentlemen anything else before we land? It's your last chance before the warning lights come on."

"No thanks. We're fine," and he made his way back to the seat, with the curious uncle asking, "What's up?"

"Nothing much," he whispered in his ear, "they will have a welcoming committee at the gate to meet us."

"Who?"

He whispered even lower. "The Feds."

He seemed disappointed. "Oh."

The three federal officers looked stern as they waited at the gate for the two police officers. They had been given physical descriptions of both men and had no difficulty in picking them out, especially the old inspector with his full head of silver hair. As they watched them approach, the short, bald one said to the other two, "That's Inspector Guilbert, the older man. He was a legend in his prime. He's cracked some tough ones. We've heard of him from the New Orleans office," and they moved forward with the incoming passengers staring at the official looking threesome, especially the one wearing the DEA jacket. One matron was heard to say as the trio went up to the duo, "Oh, look, they're going to arrest those two men who were on the plane with us! It just goes to show, you can never tell. They looked so normal, especially the older man. He looks like he could be someone's grandfather, doesn't he?"

With introductions completed, the short, bald, agent asked, "Would you gentlemen be so kind as to show us your ID's? We have to be sure you are who you're supposed to be." Having been satisfied on that score, he asked, "Do you fellows want to go to your hotel, first? We have made reservations for you at a Motel Six near our office," and as the two men looked at each other, the agent continued, "We wanted you to stay at the new Windsor Court, but your Captain Monohan said no, since the NOPD was picking up the tab, 'Motel Six would do.' What could I say?"

The old inspector grinned. "You could have said, 'screw you, Monohan,'" and they all laughed, with the agent replying, "Next time, I'll know better. Well, what did you decide? The motel, or, are you ready to go to work?"

The two men exchanged glances, and with a nod from the uncle, the nephew replied, "We're ready to go to work. Is he at your offices?"

The agents exchanged glances, shaking their heads, with the large man answering, "No, this canary is too hot to have him in our offices. There are too many people in this town who would like to cut his balls out about now and shove them down his throat. He has busted the Garaci's family's asses wide open. This is the biggest canary singing job since Joe Valachi a few years back."

The two NOPD officers nodded. "Where is he, then?" asked the nephew.

Without answering the question, the DEA man replied, "We'll take you there. He's in seclusion with his wife and baby. He is officially in the witness protection program, at his specific request."

The two New Orleans officers looked at each other, then, the nephew asked in astonishment, "Did you say wife and baby? You mean *his* wife and baby?"

"Yeah, why is that so surprising?"

He shrugged. "We just didn't know."

They were led down an escalator and to a door secured with an armed guard wearing "DEA" emblazoned on his jacket. The men nodded to him, and in recognition, nodded in return, opening the door with an electronic card. They were escorted to a waiting van with DEA emblazoned on its sides. The large agent relieved them of their carry-on bags and throwing them in the rear of the van, opened the rear door and motioned them to enter. They settled down in the rear seat, expecting a long ride, but the van was waved through several checkpoints and eventually arrived at the general aviation section of the airport, where a Sikorsky S-60, with U.S. COAST GUARD markings on its sides was waiting. The huge rotor blades were already turning, in expectation of their arrival. They were motioned to a bank of seats in the rear, and told to strap themselves in, and without further conversation, the big chopper lifted off the tarmac.

The two New Orleans officers gave each other quizzical looks, shrugging, then the nephew could contain his curiosity no longer. Over the noise of the chopper engine and blades, he tapped the large man on the shoulder, "Where the hell are we going?"

He grinned. "We're going out to the swamp; to a cabin the DEA keeps

Summary Justice

out there. They use it for surveillance of incoming drug flights and drops in the area. You'll like it," and he turned to the front again.

Not to be deterred, the nephew asked, "But I thought we were going to talk to Gino LaRoca?"

"You are," he said, without turning around.

The helicopter was maneuvering for a landing on a camouflaged helipad, hardly discernible even on a clear day, with the inspector remarking, "I'll bet that baby is hard to find at night or in bad weather."

The DEA man nodded. "That's the idea."

As the chopper got closer to the ground they could see a sprawling, one-story, wooden structure, of natural wood siding and shingles, yet, nearly obscured by cypress trees which had been allowed to stand near the camp and in various recesses and offsets, forming in itself, a natural form of camouflage to break the outline of the building from the air. No power or telephone wires could be seen leading to it, but a generator could be heard running in an out-building.

The two New Orleans officers stepped to the ground, looking around, with the nephew remarking, "Whew, this place is hard to find if you don't know where it is", and looking for roads, which were non-existent, added, "and even harder to get to."

The old inspector, looking around, asked, "Is he here?"

They all nodded. "He's here, with his wife and baby," replied the big man, "and they will stay here until he makes his appearance before the grand jury, and then we'll move him to a more permanent place until the trial. His wife is raising hell about being here, now; can't blame her. It's a hell of a life for a woman and child ... nothing to do all day ... "

He nodded. "Well, I guess he made that decision as being the best of a bad lot of choices in his position. Why did he decide to turn state's evidence? Were you about to pull him in?"

"Yeah, the whole deal was about to cave in and he knew it. He's a very smart and sophisticated man. You'll be impressed with him. He's no typical Mafia hoodlum believe me."

As they neared the compound, they could see armed guards everywhere, trying to remain unobtrusive, but there, regardless.

The inspector whistled. "You guys are taking no chances with this man, are you? I see armed men everywhere."

The agent shook his head, "No, Inspector, we have a man in there who can put the whole Garaci family behind bars for the rest of their lives, and we don't intend to let anything happen to him."

The inspector grinned, "And all he expects in return is to be allowed to live out his life in peace and quiet, huh?"

The agent nodded. "That's about it. It is a good deal; for him and for the government. He'll save Uncle Sam millions in not having to track these bastards down for the next few years, because that is about what it would have taken to get them all into court with a strong case. The same thing for your case in New Orleans. He has told us he can lay that one out for you, too."

The inspector smiled. "That is most interesting, but he will deny us the pleasure of doing it ourselves."

The agent laughed. "Well, we can always tell him to keep that information to himself, if that is what you guys want."

"No, we'll let him have his say, first."

They entered the foyer of the compound and were waved in the direction of a larger room adjoining it, where they could see a man and woman sitting on the couch, watching TV. The woman was breast-feeding a small baby when she heard the men enter. She immediately ceased the feeding, covered her breast, stood, said something to the man, and headed for another room, taking the baby with her.

The man stood and watched the entire group come in. He managed a weak smile as he saw the two men he had never seen before. As Mike Fortier would describe him later to Cindy, "He was a handsome guy, over six feet tall, with a beautiful head of black hair, just turning gray at the temples. He seemed to be about forty years old, with a great athletic build. Hell, he was impressive; not what I expected to see at all. You know, we have a preconceived idea what a Mafioso should look like ... like Jo-Jo Terrafina, but not this guy."

The DEA man made the introductions. "Gino, this is Sergeant Mike Fortier of the New Orleans Police Department, and this is his uncle, Inspector Alcide Guilbert of that department. Gentlemen, Gino LaRoca." The FBI men had gone to another room of the compound and were not present, feeling they could add nothing to the meeting. The men shook hands, with Gino LaRoca asking, "Are you the officers in charge of the New Orleans investigation of the Gervais and Barre' killings?"

They both nodded, with the inspector adding, "And the Terrafina killing, also."

Gino shrugged his shoulders, as if not interested in the latter. He turned to the DEA man. "This might take a few hours, Mr. Turner. Do you mind if I talk to my wife, first?" and turning to the New Orleans detectives, "I hope you have no need to talk to my wife. She knows nothing of the family business, and she is very upset. It has affected her supply of milk and she is having trouble feeding the baby."

The two officers looked at each other for concurrence, then, from the nephew, "No, that won't be necessary, Mr. LaRoca."

"I appreciate that," and to the DEA man, "where do you want to do this?"

He nodded toward a small office. "In there. The room has taping capabilities, and I'm sure these gentlemen will want to record your testimony, Gino."

The nephew nodded, extracting a small recorder from his pocket. "We brought our own."

The agent shook his head. "You won't get the quality from that little thing that you will from our equipment."

CHAPTER TWELVE

Having returned from speaking to his wife, he exited the room and closed the door. He shook his head, as if to himself, giving an impression to the men waiting that he was a troubled man and the talk with his wife had not gone well. He looked at them, gave them a weak smile and walked back into the office. As they watched him come forward, they both noticed that he was casually but fashionably dressed in designer slacks and a shirt. He walked with an assured gait, like a man accustomed to having his own way, previously.

He went to a chair which had a small table in front of it, as if accustomed to the routine. Mike Fortier and Alcide Guilbert sat in chairs facing him, and the DEA man sat on a chair against the wall, some distance away. For a while, no one spoke, then Gino LaRoca cleared his throat, gave them a weak smile, and said, "I guess I should tell you gentlemen what you've come all this way to hear, huh?" He spoke in a modulated voice, controlled, with near-perfect enunciation. He looked at the DEA man and raised his hands. "I'm sorry, Tom, you have to listen to all this all over again, but I only know one way to tell it, although what I have to tell these gentlemen is somewhat different from what I told you people. I'll try to confine my remarks to the New Orleans affair, and will be forced into redundancy only when the details overlap, which is unavoidable."

The DEA man smiled, saying, "Do what you have to do, Gino."

He looked at the two detectives. "I feel it is necessary to go into some background on myself, and the family, of course, if I am to have any credence in this matter ... in your eyes. I'm sure you view me as a hoodlum simply because I worked for the Garaci family, even though I only performed legal work." He smiled, "I assure you that I have never carried a gun nor have I ever blasted anybody away. There were others to do that, better equipped than I, both temperamentally and psychologically.

"Let me tell you a little about myself and perhaps you will better understand why and how I am able to do what I am doing, which is squealing on my relatives and friends. I did not choose my career. It was chosen for me, almost from the time I could speak. As you probably know, there were four Garaci brothers, all sons of the old boy who came over from Sicily in the early part of this century. The brothers were, in order of their births: Andrea (Andrew), Carlo (Charles), Pietro (Peter), and Giovanni (John). In case you don't recall, the eldest was killed in a gang war some years ago when the family was trying to consolidate the territory after Meyer Lansky was sent to Italy. I am the son of a Garaci daughter.

"When my father died young, my uncle Carlo became the head of the family. I suppose you are aware that Italian families go strictly on chronological order, unless there is a compelling reason not to. Well, my uncle Carlo took over the responsibility for my education. My mother, being a good Mafioso wife, while not relishing the idea, made no audible objections. Uncle Carlo, who had trouble with the law all his life decided that what this family needed was a lawyer—its own lawyer, so he sent me to Colombia Law School, from which I graduated cum laude. Needless to say, even though he was not sure what cum laude meant, Uncle Carlo was proud of me.

"Fortunately for me, about that time, the family began to make so much money from the drug trade that money laundering became a major problem, and instead of doing the dirty jobs like trying to come up with a defense when one of the family soldiers was caught raping some young girl, or breaking the legs of someone who was behind in his payments in loan sharking or protection, well, I was assigned to the relatively clean task of running the money laundering operation, if that makes my hands any cleaner in your eyes," and he raised and rotated his hands.

The two New Orleans detectives shifted in their chairs, so anxious were they to hear what they had come to learn, but they felt he had to go through this purging of the conscience, as he said, to lend credence to his testimony. He continued, "I know you're eager to hear about Debra Barre' and Marcel Gervais, but it is easier to me if I say it all in the sequence in which it happened, and it will make more sense." He smiled. "Remember, I'm an attorney and it is as if I were pleading my case to a jury. I know you're most anxious to hear about Debbie," and he paused, looking at the floor. It was obvious to both men that he was having trouble with this, as he continued. "I met her about five years ago when she had just come out to Miami from Louisiana. She was about twenty-seven years old then, and my God, she was beautiful ... so beautiful," and he shook his head. "Her marriage had just broken up and she was just trying to get away, to start a new life for herself, or so she told me the first night we met. She had come to a party with a man I know, a lawyer friend of mine who had the bad habit of consuming more liquor than his body and brain could accommodate. He got quite drunk, too drunk to drive, and she knew it. He had introduced us some time earlier and we had talked only a few minutes," and he smiled, more so to himself as he reminisced. He was obviously enjoying remembering a pleasant experience.

"Well, as the evening drew to a close and people were beginning to start for home, or whatever," he shrugged, "Debbie came up to me and said, 'Are you married, Gino?' I replied that I was not, and she said, 'Then you won't mind driving me home, will you? My date is drunk out of his mind.' I told her I'd be delighted to drive her home. Like any man I was egotistical enough to believe that she intended to make a night of it, but," and he shook his head, "I could not have been more wrong. When I pulled up at the curb in front of an apartment she shared with a girlfriend, she gave me one of those coy looks I got to know so well. She said, 'Gino, I hope you're not expecting a reward for this little favor. If you are, I'm willing to pay for the gas, that's all,' and she extended her hand to be shaken." He looked from one man to the other, then down at the floor. "I guess I fell in love with her at that moment. Can you imagine the moxie of that little girl telling me something like that in those circumstances? If Debbie had been a man, they would have said she had balls."

The two officers shifted in their chairs. They both felt this was going too slow. They wanted to know who had done it, and he had not said so, and he seemed to be in no hurry to tell. It was as though he were an actor on a stage, playing a part in this drama of life and he had to speak the lines as the play was written. They nodded toward him.

Sensing their impatience, he gave them a sheepish look. "I hope I'm not taking too much time with this but it should be told in its proper sequence to make sense."

The DEA agent, who had said nothing as yet, stood. "I don't mind the time, Gino, if these gentlemen from New Orleans don't, but we have to make a decision about now. Its almost dark and we have to decide if we're gonna take that chopper back to Miami, tonight, or not. The Coast Guard will want to know so they can account for it in their logs," and turning to the two police officers, "What do you gentlemen want to do? Do you want to call it a night and come back out in the morning, or go on with this thing tonight? It's up to you. I don't think Gino gives a damn. He isn't going anywhere."

The two officers looked at the troubled man, with the old inspector asking, solicitously, "What do you want to do, Gino? You look like you could use some rest."

He shrugged, "I won't sleep even if I go to bed. I would prefer to go on while I have it all arranged in my mind."

Summary Justice

The inspector turned to the DEA man. "How late can we get out of here?"

He raised his hands. "There's no time limit if we notify the Coast Guard that we'll come out late. We can call them on our satellite phone but we'll have to code the message so the drug boys who monitor everything won't know what we're talking about. So, if that's what you folks want, I'll take care of it," and he walked out.

Gino asked, "Have you fellows had anything to eat? I'm not hungry, but I can ask Terri, my wife," and he nodded toward the room at the end of the hall, "to fix you a snack, or something."

The two men, after exchanging glances, shook their heads, with the nephew saying, "No, thanks anyway. Let's get on with it."

He nodded, as he uncrossed his long legs and recrossed them in the opposite direction. "Well, let's see, where was I ... oh, yes ... Debbie. As I was saying, she let me know straight on there would be no reward for my driving her home, not what any man would hope for, anyway. As she said this, she looked me straight in the eyes. There was a street light on the opposite side of the street from us, and it made her eyes ... those dark Cajun eyes ... dance in the reflection. That creamy skin, framed by that mass of dark brown hair." He shook his head as if trying to rid himself of her memory. "I replied to her moxie statement, 'No, Miss Barre', I don't expect any reward except that you might have dinner with me one night so we can get to know each other better.' She smiled. 'What do you do for a living, Gino?' I'm a lawyer, I replied, and she said, 'Do you make a lot of money? I don't want to waste my time on a man who is a loser.' Can you believe she said that? I said to her, how much money are you interested in before you find me charming enough to date? She said, 'Depends on how I feel about a man. If I find you interesting enough, money won't matter, but if not, it will take plenty of money to keep me interested.'" He looked at them, saying, "I'm telling you all this to establish the fact that she was interested in money right from the start. She made no bones about it," and he sighed as he added, "and it was money that was her undoing."

The inspector inquired, "You brought her into the rackets, didn't you?"

He shook his head. "No, I didn't. She brought herself into it."

"Would you mind elaborating on that. I feel that this is important to our understanding the woman and the role she played in all this."

He nodded. "I guess I don't have to explain to you men that the big money nowadays is in drugs. In the old days, when I was a young man, the family made its money in the old standbys, you know, prostitution, protection, labor unions, numbers, and gambling, but all that is peanuts compared to the drug trade. When America acquired its taste for drugs, and I might add that it is an acquired taste—it was promoted and developed—the main families in the country turned to the drug trade, especially after the federal government chased most Italians out of Las Vegas and Atlantic City." He laughed, "It's tough for anyone with an Italian name to file an application with the gaming commissions."

The nephew, getting nervous, "But, Debra ... ?"

He looked contrite. "I'm sorry when I have to digress, but, let's see ... oh, yes, the drug money. There is so much cash that comes into the hands of drug people, especially at the top echelons, that it literally gets to be a burden. You have to find some way to get the stuff into the legal streams of commerce so it can make more money. Remember, if you just keep in it cash, not investing it, and with inflation running at, let's say, five percent, then your buying power diminishes by that amount, which means if you kept a dollar under your mattress for twenty years, it would be worthless at the end of that time. That's an extreme example, I know, but it's true, so the drug world had to devise means of getting the money back into commerce." He raised his hands. "I'm sure you know all this and I apologize for being redundant. Well, we used couriers to carry money back and forth between here and our suppliers in South and Central America, and it would surprise you how creative we have become in that regard.

"I've already given the DEA people a complete rundown on that, and since you're not in that end of the business, I won't bore you with it, except to tell you how Debbie fit in. After we had lived together for about a year, and she had hounded me to let her get in on some of the action, I still resisted. Not that I didn't trust her enough—I did, implicitly, but I just didn't want her to get involved. It's a dangerous game and I loved her too much." He laughed, as he remembered the incident. "I had to send her to Columbia, one time, on some paperwork business, nothing shady or illegal. Not on the surface, anyway. Well, I met her at the airport and suggested that we go to a restaurant for a good meal and some drinks. She said, 'No, I can't. Not now, anyway. Let's go home, I want to show you what I have between my legs.'" He smiled. "I said, hell, Debbie, can't that wait? We have all night for you to show me that, I joked." She shook her head, 'No sweetheart, it's not what you think,' so I took her home. She took my hand and led me into the bathroom. She lifted her skirt, which was one of those tropical types you see down in the islands, you know, full and flowing, and she laughed as she pointed to a kilo of cocaine strapped to each inner thigh.

"I was furious with her, asking her, Are you crazy, Debbie? She shrugged it off. 'It was simple,' she boasted. 'You'd be amazed what a good-looking woman can get away with. All it takes is a warm smile, a pat on the arm, and their libido takes over and their official duties suffer from it,' But, I asked, What if you run into a woman custom officer? She giggled. 'That might present a problem.'"

The nephew inquired, "And so, from that time on, she became a courier for you people, carrying money and drugs. Did she ever get on the stuff?"

He shook his head. "No, never! She was too smart for that."

The uncle asked, "I would imagine that she began to make some big money about that time, did she not?"

He shrugged. "Small by our standards, but big by hers, I guess. She was satisfied, and she was happy, or so she led me to believe."

"And you two were living together all that time, sharing an apartment, were you not?"

He nodded. "To go back in time to our first meeting, we had our first date, then a second, and on the third date, she spent the night with me, at my place. I had a fairly nice place overlooking Biscayne Bay and she was highly impressed with it. Before long, she moved in, bag and baggage." He stood up, pacing for a while, then, he turned to the two men.

"We fell madly in love, both of us," and he returned to his chair, dropping into it, wearily, asking, "Did you ever meet a woman who got into your blood? Debbie got into mine, I don't mind telling you that," and he looked at the floor, twisting his hands.

It was obvious to the two policemen that he had never gotten over the dead woman, in spite of the wife and child in the bedroom, not far from him. The nephew asked, "How long did you and Miss Barre' live together?"

He pondered the question, forming an answer, "About three years, I think. I begged her to marry me, and she almost agreed, and then she began to cool off."

The old inspector asked, "By that time, she surely knew what you did for a living," and not happy with his question, he amended it to, "I meant who you worked for."

"Oh, yes, after a while, I had no secrets from her. She knew everything about the whole operation. You couldn't keep anything secret from Debbie. She was too smart. She worked in my office as my executive assistant. We were together night and day in those days."

From the old inspector, "But, as much as she apparently loved you, she would not consent to marry you. Why?"

He shrugged. "Her biological clock was ticking, and she began to get the urge to have a baby. We discussed it, and I told her I was willing if she was. I should have known better than to discuss that with her after a romantic session, if you know what I mean. Women can get difficult when they are post-coital," and as he looked at them he said, "I guess you've found out. Well, she got real defensive about the thing, saying in an agitated manner, 'You don't think I would have a baby without being married, do you?' and when I said, no, I don't believe in that either, so let's get married, she said, 'No!, I'll never marry you as long as you're in the rackets. I don't want my child growing up in all this turmoil.' Then, after she had calmed down she added, 'if you get out of the rackets, I'll marry you, I promise.' I told her I couldn't do that. I owed too much to my family, especially my uncle. Her eyes bore into me as she asked, 'More than you owe me, Gino?' I tried to mollify her, to make her see a compromise, some kind of arrangement, but she was adamant about that. She told me she had to go on with her life ... that she was moving back to Louisiana. She asked me to make some connections for her. I took her to New Orleans and I made one of the biggest mistakes of my life, and hers. I introduced her to that asshole, Jo-Jo Terrafina."

"So, it was you who introduced Debra Barre' to the New Orleans Terrafina family."

He seemed offended. "No, I never meant for her to get into the rackets in New Orleans. We never thought much of those Terrafinas, but you know how the business is run. You reach an accommodation with a lot of people you don't care for ... just to maintain the continuity of service to the dealers. After all, one family, no matter how well organized, can't service an entire country. It takes organization."

The old uncle was getting impatient as his arthritis and hemorrhoids both bothered him from all the sitting. "Mr. LaRoca how about Marcel Gervais ... did you ever meet him? Did you introduce him to Miss Barre'?"

He seemed surprised. "No, I never met the man. Debbie met him on her own. I might tell you, now, that she and I maintained close contact after she moved to Louisiana because, in effect, she still worked for us, as a commission agent on loans."

It was the nephew who expressed surprised. "But, I thought she worked for Jo-Jo Terrafina. He said so."

She worked out of his office, for obvious reasons, since the Terrafinas also had large sums of money to launder from the stuff coming into New Orleans from the Gulf of Mexico. I have explained to the DEA boys that they have a sieve in that area like you wouldn't believe. More stuff comes in on some of those oil company supply boats then you would imagine, especially since the oil bust of recent years."

"You say you've given the DEA information on that?"

"Yes, quite a bit, but back to Debbie. She had no use for Jo-Jo. She

Summary Justice

admitted she had a brief affair with him at first, which pissed me off to no end. Debbie had no business fooling with that garlic-loving, foul-smelling ... " and he searched for words befitting his professional demeanor ... "horse's ass."

The two men smiled, with the nephew joking, "So, you've met Jo-Jo, I see."

"Yes, he came to Miami to meet with us on several occasions. I had no use for him."

The old inspector, still impatient, "But Marcel Gervais? How did they meet, he and Debra Barre'?"

"Ah, yes, the meat of the matter is it not? That's the main interest you gentlemen have in this thing. Well, Debbie called me one day and asked if she could meet with me the next day if she flew to Miami. I might tell you that I was not married, then, but going with my wife, just so you will not think I'm a bigger bastard than you already do. I lied and told her I had to go to New Orleans and I would be happy to fly there the next day, which I did. I had a room at the Westin, a lovely suite overlooking the river, and she met me there." He grinned. "That trip lasted several days because she spent the time with me ... night and day," he smiled, "But, I digress. She told me of the gambling laws passed by the Louisiana legislature and that some big projects were planned. She wanted some of the action, and knowing Debbie as I did, there was no doubt in my mind she intended to get some of it. She asked me for authority to negotiate with someone on a large deal, big money, perhaps fifty to one hundred million, she said.

"I asked her for specifics before I could commit that kind of money, and told her, further, that I would have to discuss that with the board ... we do have a board, you know," he added.

"She told me she had heard rumors that a very prominent New Orleans architect had a big deal he was trying to put together and he had run into some financing troubles, and she felt she could do business with him because she had found out he was desperate for financing, and willing to pay big interest for the money. That, of course, was precisely what we looked for, usually. We had no intention of competing with banks. We couldn't afford to. We had too many middle men who got their cuts before the money ended up in a bank in the Caymans, a legitimate bank which we own."

The two officers exchanged glances. Gino stood. "I could use a break. Would you like a coke, or something? They don't provide anything stronger than that in this government hospitality station," he joked. Both men nodded, yes, with the uncle asking, "Where's the john?"

CHAPTER THIRTEEN

As they sipped their coke, the inspector looked at his watch, eager to resume their conversation, "You were saying ... about Marcel and Debbie ... "

He nodded. "Yes, she felt confident she could get to see this gentleman, Marcel Gervais. Incidentally, before I left New Orleans, I did some of my own checking on him, because I knew the board would ask. Well, I found his credentials impeccable. He was a highly respected and successful architect, ran a big firm, and had a rich wife. He had connections at City Hall and in Baton Rouge. The deal looked good to me, and upon returning to Miami, I told the board that. They agreed to a total of one hundred million—ninety million for construction and ten million for architect's fees."

The two men looked at each other, saying nothing about the fees, but the inspector inquired, "And she evidently was successful in meeting Marcel Gervais and getting him to agree to the loans."

"Yes, she met him and proposed the loan. She told me he squealed like a stuck pig about the interest rate. Said he had a rate of nine percent quoted from the banks, and he felt that fifteen percent for thirty year money was too much."

"What did she answer to that?"

He laughed. "You have to know Debbie, as I've said before. She told me she looked him in the eye and said, 'Well, why don't you take the nine percent bank loan then? I would if I were you,' and she laughed as she added, 'Hell, Gino, honey, I knew he had lost his bank loan. It was all over town, especially in business circles, so I finally convinced him that we were the only game in town, but he was curious about the money. Where did it come from? He didn't want any dirty money. He couldn't afford that kind of deal, not with his reputation, and all that crap, so I said to him, Mr. Gervais, why don't you go with me to the Cayman Islands and talk to the bankers there who will make the loan ... would that satisfy you? He thought about that for a moment and said, 'Why yes, Miss

Barre', I think that is a good idea.' Well, after getting approval from us to take him to the Caymans she arranged the trip. She called him and asked if Mrs. Gervais would be making the trip. He said no, that she was far too busy with all her activities, so they went alone, just Debbie and Gervais."

He paused as he collected his thoughts, then, "Gentlemen, I don't know if you have spent much time in the tropics, but to sit out on a hotel balcony on a moonlit night, with the likes of Debra Barre', and watch the breezes play with her hair, and to see the moonlight reflect off the water and onto her eyes. If you can resist that, you're one hell of a man, believe me, for I have been in that situation with her on many occasions and it will drive a man crazy with desire for her, and Gervais desired her ... plenty. They spent that night together, and after that, he was a man enamored. He wanted the loan ... and her."

"Did she ever tell you that Marcel Gervais was in love with her, that he actually professed his love for her?"

"On the contrary, he did not. I asked her point blank. As I told you, later on our relationship turned to one of very close friends, although as you might have guessed by now, I never got her out of my blood. Anyway, I asked her if the man loved her, and she said no ... he had never said so except in the heat of passion, not in the cold gray of dawn, as she put it."

"Did she give you the impression that she was in love with him?"

He examined his finger nails. "Yes, that's what caused all her problems. She fell in love and lost her normally good judgment. She allowed him to do things he had no business doing, and it got them both in trouble, big trouble."

The two officers felt, that at long last, he was getting to the meat of the matter. The uncle said, "Please go on, and try to be explicit on the details."

He seemed to be searching his own mind for the correct sequence of events. "I don't know if you have access to the Gervais records or files. I may not be clear on all this, myself, but I think I have the main things correct. Gervais talked Debbie into an advance of five million for architectural fees, and she passed the request on to us. We balked at this. We were not stupid even though we dealt in easy money. I might have to digress here for just a moment to tell you about our money and how it is handled. It starts out fairly sloppy at first because it all comes in from the street dealers in five, tens, twenties, and hundreds.

"It is difficult to keep track of it, quite frankly, and a lot of it spills out the bucket, so to speak. It is not until it gets into our accounting system and the CPA's and the MBA's get into it that we really get a handle on it, but after that, our accounting is as good as a bank's. It was in that spilling stage, early in the game, that Debbie learned a lot of bad habits, because she found ways to skim off the top when she was a courier and hiding it in her favorite hiding place—between her legs. I tried to warn her about this, but she laughed it off with the 'beautiful woman' thing I told you about."

He took a deep breath. "Well, anyway, we balked at the huge advance Gervais had requested. We even checked with architectural firms in the Miami area, and found that a retainer of sorts would be acceptable, but not half the fee. He still balked, and we found out why later in our investigation of the matter. He was in big trouble on an oil well drilling venture and his partners were about to come down on his head. He could not afford the bad publicity, we found out."

The nephew inquired, "And Debra knew about the oil well venture, did she not?"

He shook his head. "Not at first, not from what she told me, anyway. That was the basic problem. Because of her love for him, he began to force her to agree to things she had no business agreeing to, and it got her into trouble."

The two officers noticed that that was the second time he made reference to "getting her into trouble. Making her do things she had no business doing."

"You've made that statement on two occasions, Gino, that Marcel Gervais *made* Debra do something she should not have done," asked the uncle, "could you tell us what you mean by that?"

He sat silent for a while, thinking out his response. "As I told you, Debbie was a smart cookie ... street smart, as they say. Under normal conditions, in a routine business deal, no man would have been able to make her do something against her better judgment, but she fell for Gervais, and that started her problem ... "

"Such as? Be specific, please."

"Well, she loaned him over two hundred thousand dollars to put in the oil well venture after he got his tail in a big crack, and that money is gone, believe me."

"But," contested the uncle, "why should that bother you or the family. It was her money, made from the ten percent commission Gervais had paid her from his draws."

He stood up, pacing, obviously agitated at that remark. "Don't you see, that was the basic problem. Debbie was double dipping! We had already paid her a commission on the amount they would draw. That was the basic agreement on any loan she placed for us. Her commission was ten percent. It had been for years, and as long as she lived with me and I could keep an eye on her, the deal worked fine." He shook his head from side to side, as if the memory of it still bothered him greatly. "But when she got to New Orleans on her own, her inherent greed took hold. She played both ends against the middle. She convinced Gervais that she always received a ten percent commission on her draws, which is not precisely correct. She had talked him into signing a counter letter to that effect."

The inspector raised his hands, asking the question, "But, why should that offend your group? If Gervais was stupid enough to pay her that kind of money on top of what your group had paid her, then, he is the stupid one."

"No, no, you don't understand the situation," he argued, "by taking out ten percent of his money, she was stealing it from the project. If the deal had gone through, by the time we had disbursed ninety million for construction and ten million for fees, which is what the agreement called for, the project would have been short ten million dollars, because she would have been paid her ten million by Gervais," he said, tapping the arm of the chair for emphasis.

The two police officers whistled, with the nephew exclaiming, "And that would have been on top of the ten million you people paid her."

"No, that is not correct. She would have made nowhere near ten million on her commission with us ... "

"But, you just said your people paid her ten percent."

"Yes," he nodded, "it started at ten, but it was on a graduated scale from then on. As the amount goes up, her percentage comes down ... way down. There's no way we would have paid her a full ten percent fee on that big loan."

The cynical old inspector grunted. "Perhaps, Marcel Gervais should have been that wise. I can't believe he agreed to pay that young woman a full ten percent commission."

"Oh, don't feel sorry for him, Inspector. He knew what he was doing all the time, at least, after he had determined that Debbie was in love with him. He used her."

"What do you mean?"

The attorney shrugged his shoulders and let them sag. It was obvious that the ordeal was beginning to take a toll on him, as he replied, "We now know, for sure in some cases, and we surmise in others, that he intended to get all the money back in one form or another. You will recall that he borrowed over two hundred thousand from her to put into that rat hole of an oil deal, and he hoped to get hundreds of thousands more from her on the Esperante project."

"But, how?"

"Poor kid. She called me all excited, one night. She said, 'Gino, guess what? Marcel has agreed to make me a silent partner in the Esperante project. At last, Gino, I'm having a chance to strike it big,' and when I didn't respond for a moment while I went over the ramifications in my own mind, she asked, 'What's the matter, honey? Aren't you happy for me?' I said to her, " Debbie, baby, don't do this. You're going to get your beautiful ass in big trouble ... big trouble. Those were my exact words to her."

"What did she say?"

He shook his head. "She took offense at it. Screamed at me, 'You're just jealous at my success. You're still pissed because I wouldn't marry you, that's your problem, Gino.' I tried to argue with her, but she told me her mind was made up, and she asked me the most important question she had ever asked me in her entire life, and I gave her the wrong answer," and he looked down at the floor, shaking his head.

The inspector said, softly, "I bet I can tell you what the question was, Gino," and as the attorney looked up, waiting for the answer, the inspector continued, "she asked you if you were going to spill the beans to the board, right?"

He nodded, without answering audibly, with the inspector saying, "And that is what you meant when you said he got her in all kinds of trouble, wasn't it?"

He rubbed his hands, nodding from one man to the other.

The inspector continued his grilling. "There's one thing I don't understand, Gino, and I wish you'd clear it up, because it is bugging me," and as the attorney raised his head, "How were you able to know so much about what Debbie and Marcel Gervais were up to? I don't understand that."

He sighed, "Well, as I told you, she and I had maintained a very close relationship after she moved to New Orleans. She told me everything. She always did, until we had that blow up I just told you about, and even then," he smiled, "she called me the next night, crying over the phone, telling me how sorry she was for what she had said ... asked me to forgive her ... "

"And you did, huh?"

"Hell, I always did. She knew that I still loved her, and I always would ... she knew it."

The inspector rose to stretch his legs, and standing in front of the attorney, he asked in a fatherly tone, "Gino, tell me. Did you inform the board of her deception? I'd like to know, because I feel it has a lot to do with her death."

He looked at the floor for a while, then out the window at the darkening sky, pointing his finger, "No, my conscience is clear on that, but it made no difference. They found out."

"But, how?"

"You know that little corporation she set up to conduct her 'consulting business', as she called it ... "

"You're referring to Golden Meadow Resources, are you not?"

"That's the one. On my advice, she had it set up as a foreign corporation, in the Caymans. Hell, I set it up for her. The account was with our bank, Banco Del Mar. As I told you, previously, we owned it, we controlled it—lock, stock, and barrel." He took a deep breath, adding, "I told you a while back that our accounting was sloppy at the lower end. It had to be with the low lifes we were dealing with, but I also told you that once it got into our pipeline, where the CPA's and the MBA's got hold of it, we ran a very tight ship, especially on anything that came through our bank."

He smiled a contrite smile. "Poor Debbie, as smart as she was, she apparently never thought about our people perusing her checks as they came through her account, but they did. It didn't take them long to figure out what was going on. They knew how much we paid her, and when they saw those checks for the Esperante partnership, especially for her shares, well, the red flag went up ... on her and Marcel Gervais.

"The board sent a team to New Orleans to check it out. The team included architects and engineers from the Miami area, and they insisted that Marcel Gervais show them the progress he had made on the project. He took them to his office at night when no one else was around and he gave them a horse-and-pony show like you wouldn't believe. Incidentally, he had not been told that there was an architect and engineer in the group. He showed them models and drawings of what he claimed were the studies for the project. The only trouble was he showed them renderings of the same study done from different angles and with different variations ... pure bullshit ... and he thought the laymen would never catch it, and they wouldn't have, but the professionals did. When they got back to Miami, they informed our board that they could not see even a hundred thousand dollars of work there, much less the two million Gervais had drawn.

"Well, things began to deteriorate very fast after that visit. Now believing that something stunk badly, they launched a full-blown investigation of the project and Debbie's hand in it. They monitored her bank accounts, as I've said before, and in time, they had a good case against Debbie and her lover, Gervais.

"They called me in on the carpet, knowing full well that Debbie was a creature of my making. They were well aware, of course, of our relationship both here in Miami, and the continuation of it in New Orleans ... "

"Then," the inspector interrupted, "they felt you had some blame in the matter."

"Well, they didn't blame me for the Gervais fiasco, but they felt I should have reined Debbie in, but," and he shook his head, "they just didn't know Debbie like I did. She had made up her mind she was going to do this thing, and of course, after she fell in love with Gervais, there was no stopping her."

The inspector could contain himself no longer, now that he felt they were nearing the end of this drama, and they still had no idea who killed the pair, or Jo-Jo Terrafina. He gazed intently at the attorney, asking, "Gino, did the board order the killing of those people in retaliation for what they perceived as a great deception of their trust in them?"

"Yes, it was a board decision, but," and he hesitated for a moment, once again, searching for words, "you have to understand how things are run these days—with the family, that is. The old boys, the three remaining brothers are old and sick and they are retired. They don't even live in this country anymore. One lives in the Caymans and the other two live in the Bahamas."

"Who runs the family, now?"

"The sons—my cousins—but, once again, you have to understand how things are run in an Italian family. There is a pecking order based on who is whose son. Remember, I am the son of a Garaci daughter, so I am not in the forefront like my cousins, the sons of the sons," and he snorted, "Not that I wanted to be, either. I was content to be on the periphery, simply as a legal advisor and not as a full board member. I might point out that the family is completely different now than when the old boys ran it. True, they were not educated men, not cultured or sophisticated, but they had some common sense which the young boys do not. The old boys knew, instinctively, how far they could go; how far they could buck the system, and if they went any further, they knew the Feds would come down on them due to public outcry and news media provocation. But, the young turks who run the show now, although better educated than the old boys, don't have their common sense. They've watched too many movies about the old days and believe that is the way they're supposed to act. They have no finesse. They believe they are invincible."

The nephew asked, "Are you telling us you had no vote in this thing?"

"That's right, I didn't. Oh, I know how it looks. You're probably sitting there thinking, right now: sure, he'll say anything to save his ass, but remember, I'm not being charged with anything by the Feds, except being an accessory to their crimes, and I've plea bargained all that away. That is what this is all about, isn't it?"

Without answering his question, the inspector asked, "Gino, were you present at the meeting when they voted to have Debbie and Gervais killed?"

"At first, yes, but when it was discussed in my presence and when they talked about killing Debbie, too, I raised strenuous objections to that. I pleaded her case, trying to convince them that she was led into the deception by Gervais. They sat, impassively, and I could see I was making no headway, so I tried another tact. I told them I would make complete restitution for Debbie's money: the ten percent she had gotten from Gervais, and I thought this would do it. They looked at one another, nodding to each other, then, telling me, 'OK, Gino, we'll spare the broad for your sake, but we want our money back.' I stood at the table, saying, I'll pay every cent of it back. They all nodded, so I left the room, thinking it was over—a done deal—but I found out later from one of my cousins who was the closest to me, that after I left the room, my cousin, Carlo, Jr., who fancies himself the new Don, hit the table with the fist, saying, 'Kill the bitch, too.' They took a new vote and you know the rest." He suppressed a sob, turning his head toward the window.

The two policemen sat there for a while, saying nothing, mulling his words, then the inspector asked, "Gino, is that what made you come forward with all this? The killing of Debra Barre'?"

He sniffed, no longer attempting to hide his feelings. "It was two things, really ... no, actually three," and he pointed down the hall, toward the direction of the room where his wife and baby were. He went on, "I just told you about how the family was run nowadays. I couldn't see anything but a disaster coming down the road with those hot heads in control. I felt it was only a matter of time before it all blew up in our faces. I could feel it in my bones." He once again looked down the hall. "I guess it's time I talked about my wife and baby. As I told you earlier, Terri and I were going together after Debbie returned to Louisiana. She's a good kid ... not like Debbie, but I don't mean that in a derogatory sense, for Debbie was not really a bad person. She just had screwed up values, that's all. She wanted to be rich, a wheel. I guess that is what attracted her to Gervais. She told me, once, 'he's a wheel in this town.'

"Well, Terri and I had never discussed marriage ... until she turned up pregnant." He shook his head. "Hell, I guess we would never have married if it hadn't been for the baby. We talked abortion for a while, but, after thinking about it, she changed her mind. Said she wanted the baby. I thought about it. Hell, I'm forty years old, and what have I got to show for my life? So, I proposed, and we got married, and now ... "

"Did Debbie know you were married?"

"Oh, yes, I told her. She wished me luck, but to complete the answer to your question, 'why?' I agonized over this thing until I nearly went out of my mind. I felt if something didn't happen to change the course of events, I would end up going to jail for the rest of my life, and ... my wife and baby deserved better than that. What kind of legacy would I be leaving my child? What would she think of me? I hope, someday, she will understand why I'm doing what I am doing ... for her." Then, he stood and walked to the window. He stared at a sky as black as his future. Then he turned to the men, "And that last of the three reasons is Debbie. I don't guess I'll ever get her out of my system as long as I live, even though it was not meant to be. As I said, she's in my blood. I hope my wife never finds out just how much." He sat down, again, rubbing one hand against the other, as he continued, "They didn't have to kill her. The only thing she had done to annoy them was she misappropriated some money, that's all, and I had promised to pay that back, but I heard from that same cousin I mentioned earlier, they wanted to teach a lesson to anyone doing business with the family, that they tolerated no crap from anyone. But," and he shook his head, again, "they didn't have to kill her, not like that. It made her look like a cheap whore, and she was not. Debbie was a decent woman! She loved the man—that was the problem. I can understand that."

The two policemen sat quietly for a moment, respecting the man's grief, then, from the nephew, "Gino, how about Jo-Jo? Why did they kill him?"

He smirked. "They killed him for being stupid, that's why."

"What do you mean by that? If being stupid was justification for murder, there'd be more dead people in this world than there are."

"But, he raised stupidity to an art form."

"Was he involved in the Gervais thing?"

"Not at first. At least, we didn't know of it. It was only after we started the investigation of the whole thing that we found out he had formed two dummy companies to procure land in the places where he thought a gambling casino might go. It was pure coincidence, I guess, that two of the places were where Marcel Gervais had bought an option."

"But, is that a sin? Did that justify killing him? He might have made a few dollars on the deal, but that's business, isn't it?"

"Perhaps to you, but not the family. This goes way back, before the Gervais thing. Jo-Jo had alienated the family on several other deals. He had set up his own courier service on the stuff coming in from the gulf coast ... remember, I mentioned that earlier. Jo-Jo had bought five oil company cargo boats—they're for sale all over the place since the oil bust. And he had set up his own trade in competition with the stuff we had coming in through Florida, and he was supposed to be part of our operation." He took a deep breath. "They decided to send the man back and get rid of Jo-Jo, too, to clean up the whole mess. But, they didn't want it to happen on the same day. They wanted to separate the killings. They figured that so many people had a good reason to kill Jo-Jo, that the police would never solve it."

The inspector's eyes opened wide. "You said ... 'send the man back' ... what man, Gino? Who did it? Who pulled the trigger?"

He raised his hands. "I don't know who he was. Nobody in our organization knows who he is. You will never know who actually did the killing."

The inspector grew agitated. "You don't really expect us to accept that answer, do you? Why do you think we came out here all this way to talk to you?"

He moved his head from one side to the other, twitching his lips. "I'm not trying to insult your intelligence, gentlemen. I really don't know, and the family doesn't, either, believe me! They hired a contract killer from Europe. We gave up on the domestic boys years ago. They always got caught by the Feds. They hired him through a booking agent in Europe, and I know for a fact that the thing goes through several middle men, all without names; just telephone numbers, and they change those every month or so. Believe me, you will *never* know who did the actual killing ... never."

The two policemen exchanged glances, and their disappointment could not be concealed. They said nothing for several minutes, believing that what the man said was true: they would never know who pulled the trigger. They now knew why it was done, but not by whom. The inspector rose, walked to the attorney, who's face reflected the strain of the ordeal as he sat there, his handsome head lowered, his hands in his lap. The inspector placed his hand on the attorney's shoulder. "Gino, we appreciate your leveling with us. I know this has not been easy for you. I'm not sure we would have ever figured out all the answers to this puzzle, although we were getting close, but it did save us a lot of time and the taxpayers some money. Can you think of anything else we ought to know about this affair?"

He looked up, shaking his head, replying softly, "No, I've told you all I know. There's nothing left. It's all over, and, now, if you don't mind I'd like to return to my wife and baby."

The old inspector nodded, patting him on the shoulder, saying, in a fatherly fashion. "Go to them, my boy. They need you badly, I'm sure. You have a rough time ahead of you, for the rest of your life, and they have to share your destiny ... and your fate."

In a small bedroom, barely fifty feet from where the men were talking, a lovely young woman sat in a rocking chair, rocking back and forth, her head laid back on the headrest. A small infant, only two months old, suckled at her breast, grunting and squirming as it consumed the milk of life. The mother slowly lowered her gaze to the infant, then stroked the baby's sparse hair, smiling, as tears streamed down her cheeks. The tears reached her mouth. She corralled the tears with her tongue, forcing them to reenter her body. Her head went back on the headrest, moving from one side to the other as she pondered her fate and that of her child.

The men rose, thanking the dejected and morose attorney for his help, and feeling genuinely sorry for a man they now considered a decent human being, thrown into a life he had no stomach for, by reason of birth, alone. They made their way out to the waiting helicopter. The night was dark, very dark. Not only was there no moonlight, but the compound was so designed that, at night, all interior lights were shrouded from outside view. The nephew whispered to the uncle, "This place gives me the creeps. I miss the bright lights of the Big Easy, Unck."

"Yeah, me too. I'm ready to get back home," and with that they entered the noisy chopper for the return to Miami and their motel room. Neither man slept well that night for different reasons. Mike's mind was churning as he relived the entire episode in his mind, now that all the pieces of the puzzle were on the table in their proper position. The uncle snored in relative peace, a peace brought on by an acceptance of the facts. Now that they knew, his mind was at ease, even if they didn't know who the actual killer was, and he now accepted the fact they never would.

But, as the older man slept, the younger man continued to turn the thing over in his mind. "Why?" He asked himself. Why did it have to happen?" If Marcel Gervais had been satisfied to continue the life of ease and luxury he had enjoyed for over a half century, but no, he was dissatisfied, he had something eating at him. There reposed in him an artistic craving which was not being satisfied, and in his mistaken way, he believed that this was a solution- a project of his own, in which he was the master. He was driven, not by money, but by artistic craving to be recognized and honored as before.

Debra Barre' marched to a different drumbeat. If she had only gone home with her relatively good-size fortune and enjoyed the simple life down the bayou, she would still be alive. But she, too, had something eating at her. She was driven by a different urge. She wanted more money, recognition and fame that she felt her beauty and brains entitled her to.

And Jo-Jo Terrafina ... why try to explain it? He was doomed from birth ... a star-crossed birth. It was inevitable. It had to happen. It was not a matter of if, but when and where.

The next morning, as the Boeing 737 climbed to its cruising altitude, the two settled back with coffee and rolls, brought to them by the same flight attendant they had met on their flight to Miami. She immediately recognized them. Smiling her best Delta Airline smile, she asked, "Well, gentlemen, good morning. Have an interesting evening in Miami? Anything you want to talk about?" She giggled as she added, "Or, can talk about?" she teased.

The nephew accepted the coffee and rolls, handing his share to the uncle at the window seat (he always insisted on the window seat so "I can look out, that's why"), and returning his attention to the question at hand, he replied, "No, nothing interesting! I'll be happy to get back to New Orleans."

"Oh, I just love New Orleans," smiled the flight attendant as she sat on the arm of the empty aisle seat, continuing with, "I just wish I knew where to go. There's so much to see *if* you know where to go." She glanced at the ring finger of the nephew, with its telltale band of gold.

The old inspector's ears and eyes perked up like a hound dog on a scent. "What you need, my dear, is a guide. Someone who knows the city, and," he smiled, "someone you can trust. You know its so dangerous out there these days for a single woman, especially one as attractive as yourself." Warming to the subject, he changed places with the nephew, motioning him over to the window seat with a jerk of the head, he continued, "I'm retired, you know, and have a lot of time on my hands. If you wish, I would be most happy to show you around the town ... anytime."

Looking at the silver white hair and sensing him to be long past the age when ardent fire burned brightly in the cellar, she cooed, "Oh, would you? I'd love that."

He smiled a victory smile. "Why, of course, I would ... any time, my dear," and taking a pad from his jacket pocket, he wrote down his name and phone number, adding, "You can reach me at this number, day or night."

She smiled. "You'll be hearing from me, Alcide. Then, rising from the seat arm, and with a bit of female devilment she could not suppress, she placed her hand on his arm. "Oh! Do you mind if I bring my fiancé? I just got engaged, and ... "

He tried to hide his disappointment and chagrin, smiling, "No, my dear, by all means, bring him along. Dutch treat, of course," he added with a mischievous grin.

The nephew had great difficulty in not choking on his roll, as the flight attendant smiled and winked at him before leaving. He nudged the older man in the ribs. "Well, Unck, good try."

The old man smiled, philosophically, biting on his roll, "You win some, you lose some, Michael," and leaning back on the head rest, "There's always Rosalie, you know."

Summary Justice

CHAPTER FOURTEEN

MONDAY MORNING

The auditorium at City Hall in New Orleans was a bedlam of humanity as the news media from all parts of the country converged on the Crescent City to hear of the solution of the Gervais/Barre' murders. The national news media had broken the story of the defection of one Gino LaRoca of the infamous Garaci crime family operating out of Miami, and although no details had been released as yet on the New Orleans murders, an over zealous information officer in the Miami FBI office had casually mentioned that Gino LaRoca's testimony did, indeed, include the New Orleans killings.

All city officialdom was present, from the mayor to the city council to the police commissioner to the precinct captain, Monohan, who beamed proudly on his newest promotion, Lieutenant Michael Fortier. Cindy was there, as were the two Fortier children, sitting on the front row. She, too, beamed proudly at the department's newest lieutenant, and relished the role of Mrs. Lieutenant Michael Fortier. She turned to look at the rear of the room, and there, leaning against the wall, was the old, once again retired Inspector of Detectives, Alcide J. Guilbert. Cindy and Mike had both begged him to come forward, to share in the recognition ceremonies, but he grinned, "No, this is Mike's day. I don't need it." Even the pleading of his old friend, Monohan, did no good. "Come on, Alcide, don't act like a horse's ass. You know you should share in this ceremony. You know damn well that I know how you helped the kid..." His reply was, "Monohan, if you value your marriage, you will keep your big Irish mouth shut, hear me?"

The two police officers had returned from Miami on Sunday, the day before, and had made a full report to the captain, who had called the chief, who had called the commissioner, who had proudly called the mayor to announce that the Gervais case was solved. The mayor responded, "That's great! I'm proud of the department. Who did it? You don't know! What do you mean you don't know? I thought you said the damn case was solved? You'd better come over to see me, now. I'd like to know what is going on before I call the news conference tomorrow. I'd call it today, but you know we'll never get national coverage this fast, and especially on a Sunday."

It was the mayor who tapped for order and silence, and after waiting quite some time to achieve it, cleared his throat and began to read from a prepared speech. He called to everyone's attention that this baffling murder had occurred only ten days before, and although the complexity of the case was mind boggling, the department "of which we can be most proud," and he beamed at the new lieutenant sitting there in the front row with his family. He reminded those in attendance that the murder was baffling from several points of view, especially since it involved one of the city's most respected and honored citizens. He implored them, "It is not our task to judge what the victims did to deserve this fate. No, it is our duty as Christians to leave that verdict to a higher judge, who will, in turn, someday judge us all," and with that, he called to the podium, "Lieutenant Michael Fortier, the officer who was instrumental in bringing this case to a successful conclusion, to come forth and answer any questions you folks from the media might have, but before he does, I'd like to ask Lieutenant Fortier, his wife, and his children, to come to the podium where it will be my pleasure to present him with the City of New Orleans' Medal of Commendation for a job well done."

Cindy blinked back tears of pride, while the kids nervously shifted their weight from one foot to the other, each holding their mother's hand. The new lieutenant smilingly accepted the hastily arranged and framed document from his Honor, the Mayor. As he took it in hand, his eyes went to the rear of the auditorium. He saw the old inspector leaning against the wall, smiling, nodding his head. He smiled back, an all knowing smile. He blinked at the barrage of lights now aimed at him for this was a new world to him. Their questions were harsh, penetrating, callous, with no regard or respect for the feelings of the families of the victims. Marcel Gervais's lifetime of honesty and integrity was torn to shreds as the media groped for answers to questions beyond the scope of good taste.

It was merciful that the widow, Elsbeth Cartier Gervais, and her two daughters, had left town on an early flight that morning when the news broke that the case had been solved. She felt, and she had said so to her daughters, "I can conceive of no explanation to this awful affair that will not have a disastrous affect on us who loved him. The media will drag his memory through the mud as though he were a gutter rat, instead of one of the leading citizens of this community," and she sobbed ... " of this city to which he has given so much." It was as true, now, as it was when it was

Summary Justice

written so many years before, "The evil that men do lives after them ... the good is oft interred in their bones."

Mike Fortier, although uneasy and sometimes awkward, managed to answer their questions as to why, but when the all important question was asked, "WHO DID IT?" He looked at the rear of the room, as if pleading for an answer which did not come, he shook his head. "We don't know. I doubt that we will ever know, for sure," and to the protestations of the media who demanded to know who demanded revenge, he could only explain the situation as Gino LaRoca had explained it, "We know for sure it was done by an international hit man; a professional who does this for a living. That's all we know. We've turned the information over to Interpol, the International Police Organization. They will keep trying, but, that is all we can do for now," he said apologetically, and to the grumblings of those unsatisfied with that answer, the news conference came to an end.

The news media closed in on the hero of the day, asking for photographs of him, Cindy, and the children. He had his fifteen minutes of fame, which all humanity seems to be allotted in some varying degrees, and with that done, he took his wife by the arm as she held the commendation plague, and with the two children following, went to the rear of the auditorium.

The old inspector smiled as he saw them approach, and reaching for the commendation plaque, he grinned, "Well, Lieutenant, this has been quite a day for you, and I'm proud of you."

The nephew grunted, "Hell, Unck, don't pull that psychological crap on me. You know you should have been up there with me. Why are you so stubborn, sometimes?"

He grinned, "My hemorrhoids are bothering me. I think I'll go and have them removed. I'm spending too much money on Preparation H. I could buy beer with that money," and turning to Cindy, "Honey, you owe me one more meal of seafood gumbo."

She embraced him. "I know Unck. I cooked it last night. Let's go home."

CHAPTER FIFTEEN

EPILOGUE

He had driven from Madrid, deep in the heart of the Spanish nation, to the Mediterranean, to Valencia by the sea. He had at his side a Spanish beauty, with hair as black as ebony, eyes as dark and mysterious as a jungle pool, her skin the color of unpolished ivory, and her teeth, the shade of mother of pearl, and a figure to arouse the jealousy of a model. She had not come cheap, for this was her trade. She was a professional, a purveyor of love and companionship—at a price.

He didn't mind. He could afford her. This was his custom. He bought companionship and comfort on an "as-needed basis", at the going market price. Sometimes, he would quibble about the price, not to achieve a lower one, but as a means of stimulation. He enjoyed it, and he felt they did, too. Now, as he neared the coast, he informed her he would need her services no longer. She was indignant. "But, Nicalo," she pouted in her Spanish tongue, "you promised to take me with you to the Riviera ... you promised. That is why I lowered my price. Do you really think I would come with you for that sum. What do you think I am?"

He gave her a cold smile. *"You are a mercenaria ... a prostituta ... exponer a' todo genero de torpeza' y sensualidad.* You know it, and I know it, too."

She slid down in the seat of the convertible, the wind blowing her hair in her eyes. She brushed the hair back, pouting, "But, you don't have to be so explicit, do you?" She placed her hand on his right arm, smiling, "Where is all that romance you had last night, Nicalo? Is it gone, now?"

He never even returned her look, nor her touch, as he responded, coldly, "It left with the dawn."

"But," she persisted, as seductively as she could muster, "for every dawn there is a night, Nicalo, and I could be there with you ... at your side," and turning to look at the passing landscape, "Are you tired of me so soon?"

He managed a smile. "Not tired, my little one, just finished with you."

Summary Justice

"Men," she snorted, "you're all alike! You're only interested in one thing."

He finally looked at her. "When I meet a woman who has something else to offer, I will be interested in that, too."

She pouted, "Oh, Nicalo, please, take me to Monaco with you," and she tugged at his arm, causing him to swerve.

That strange mechanism that had triggered so many of his actions in his violent lifetime, snapped in his brain. He applied the brakes so fast that she nearly hit her head on the dashboard. His personality changed to one of aggression as the adrenaline began to flow. He reached over and opened the door on her side and pushed her out of the car, kicking her with his feet. She tried to resist, reaching for anything to grab on to, but her strength was no match for his. Screaming and crying, she landed on the side of the road, in the gravel. She got up, hysterical, pleading, "What are you doing? Are you crazy? What will I do out here? Please don't leave me, Nicalo. *Please,*.." but her pleading was lost in the grinding wheels and the whining of the engine. He looked back through the rear view mirror, and as he saw her waving, frantically, a cold smile crossed his lips, then he turned his attention to the winding, hilly road before him and continued on to Valencia.

He checked the car in at a rental agency, and taking his B-4 bag and the over-size briefcase, he took a taxi down to the waterfront area. He boarded a small interisland ship headed for Nice, and then, to his long awaited, and delayed vacation on the French Riviera. Upon arriving at Nice, he checked out the automobile rental agencies, and seeing one that advertised the Mercedes-Benz line, he entered there.

In French, the desk clerk asked, "May I help you, sir?"

Also in fluent French, he replied, "Yes, I would like to rent a Mercedes convertible for a month."

The clerk's eyebrows raised, noticeably, as he perused the man to ascertain if he were even capable of paying for a Mercedes convertible for a month. So many blow-hards came to the Riviera at this time of the year, he felt, students and the like, who could barely manage to afford a hotel room for one night, much less a fifty thousand dollar convertible for a month, even a used one.

He replied, coolly and professionally, "That would require a sizable deposit, Monsieur. Tres grand," he emphasized in his native tongue.

He was becoming annoyed. "And how large would that be?" and he shoved a gold Master Card across the counter, a secured card, issued by a Madrid bank.

The clerk picked up the card, perused it, and placed it in the machine slot, then, punched in some numbers, waiting to see if the amount of

Lloyd J. Guillory

credit would clear. His eyes widened and his lips pursed, as the machine clicked a response, and a slight smile crossed his face as he said, "Tres bien, Monsieur."

He headed out on the hilly and curvy coast highway leading to the French Riviera. It was a beautiful day, with an azure blue sky slightly tinted with a fuzzy haze at the horizon. The Mediterranean Sea, reflectively, transformed the azure blue sky to a lovely turquoise, shimmering in the midday sun. He ran his fingers through his hair as the warm breezes ruffled it. In his twisted mind, he was as happy as he would ever be. He felt successful. He was at the peak of his profession. His services were required and asked for on three continents, and he basked in the glow of that success, as he turned his gaze to watch two sailboats in a race about two miles offshore from the coast road. As he wheeled around a tight, blind curve, he had no opportunity to see or avoid the stalled truck in the middle of the road. The truck, loaded with chickens for the rich palates of the exclusive resort to the east, was being driven by a local farmer who was frantically waving as he stood in the middle of the road, but it was too late. The convertible was going too fast, and there were only two options open to the driver: to hit the truck, or to swerve to miss on the only open side, the ocean side, (the other side blocked by a steep hill). His eyes widened in horror as he realized his mistake. His face froze in terror as had the faces of so many of his victims as he pulled the trigger to end their lives. For some strange reason, the face of Debra Barre' crossed his mind at the same instant that the convertible left the road, crashing through the steel barrier. It bounced off one rocky cliff and another on its two-hundred foot journey to the beach below. As it was designed to do, the seat belt held fast, keeping him pinned in his chamber of death.

As the car careened down the steep slope, with his body held in place by the seat belt, his head was buffeted about, striking one object and then another, resulting in many serious wounds. As he felt himself being thrown about, his life began to flash before him. His heinous crimes which had seemed so justifiable in his twisted mind at the time and so easily done, now flashed before him as brightly as the sun in the few horrible seconds left to his life. He was still alive, but just barely. The car came to a halt on its side, with his mind wandering in and out of consciousness. He looked up at the sky as if trying to plead some heavenly assistance to avoid his end, for atheist that he was, and like all atheists at the last moment of their lives, suddenly he realized that he really was not one, after all. But his conversion came too late, and his sins were too great as he faced the greatest fear known to mankind ... the fear of the hereafter.

The peasant farmer truck driver standing at the top of the hill, witnessed the tragedy that had unfolded. In keeping with his deep faith, he made the sign of the cross, shaking his head, reciting an Act of Contrition for the departed soul.

The coroner's inquest, held the next day in Monte Carlo, listed the deceased, based on records found on his person, as one Nicola Guissepi Buonorroti. The Madrid address shown on his passport was a fake. The Madrid bank which had issued the secured credit card, carried only the fake address. Knowing of no relatives or friends to whom the body could be entrusted, the local undertaker extracted the required sum of money from his wallet, cremated the remains, and forwarded the remaining money to the local orphanage..

His over-size briefcase, when first viewed by the officials of Monaco, raised eyebrows. They turned it over to Interpol, who made many assumptions as to its purposes. Interpol checked the gun barrel markings on both the rifle and the hand gun, and those results were sent around the world, including the New Orleans Police Department laboratory.

The *Times-Picayune* ran a glaring headline GERVAIS MURDER SOLVED. ASSASSIN IDENTIFIED.

"VENGEANCE IS MINE," SAYETH THE LORD.